Principles of Adaptation for Film and Television

PRINCIPLES OF ADAPTATION FOR FILM AND TELEVISION

By Ben Brady

 University of Texas Press, Austin

Requests for permission to reproduce material from this work should be sent
to Permissions, University of Texas Press, Box 7819, Austin, TX 78713-7819.

∞ The paper used in this publication meets the minimum requirements of
American National Standard for Information Sciences—Permanence of Paper
for Printed Library Materials, ANSI Z39.48-1984.

The screenplay by Ben Brady was adapted from the novel *Claire Serrat* by
I.A.R. Wylie with permission from the Medical College of Pennsylvania.

Library of Congress Cataloging-in-Publication Data

Brady, Ben.
Principles of adaptation for film and television / by Ben Brady. — 1st ed.
  p. cm.
Includes index.
ISBN 0-292-70804-1 (alk. paper). — ISBN 0-292-70807-6 (alk. paper pbk.)
1. Film adaptations. 2. Television adaptations. I. Title.
PN1997.85.B73 1994
808.2'3—dc20
93-8798

To my lifetime partner,

Estelle,

for her wisdom, her constancy, and her love

CONTENTS

Preface   ix

Acknowledgments   xiii

Part 1. Principles of Adaptation for Film and Television   1

  1. Introduction   3

  2. The Transition   14

  3. Plot   23

  4. The Premise   30

  5. Character   35

  6. The Nature of a Treatment   42

  7. The Treatment   46

  8. Dialogue   56

  9. Camera Language and Screenplay Format   60

Part 2. The Screenplay *Claire Serrat*   69

Part 3. Questioning Your Adaptation   199

Glossary of Film Terms   207

Index   217

PREFACE

For many different reasons, authors who adapt their own books into screenplays are rare. Whether the author feels that he or she has done the job—peaked out, so to speak—or whether the producers believe that a book and a movie require different talents, an open door exists for educated screenwriters to seek out published novels that have somehow escaped the attention of the world's film market.

This is not to say that authors never adapt their own works. The screenplay for *Dances with Wolves* was written by the author. So was *GoodFellas*, as well as others. But the fact remains that film is a completely different form; it is not a celluloid version of a novel. And a writer who attempts to translate a novel into a screenplay must understand that before starting.

Thus, an equal opportunity exists for the unpublished novelist. Given the techniques provided by this book, an adaptation becomes another way of ultimately getting a story published—or produced.

Long ago I started out as a New York attorney specializing in theatrical law. It was my destiny, after ten years of practice, to transfer my entire attention to the artistic rather than the legal aspects of my clients' affairs. I spent the next twenty-five years as a writer, director, producer, and, finally, in Hollywood, vice-president in charge of programming at the American Broadcasting Company. Along the way, I founded and was president of the Television Producers Guild.

The programs I produced were among the leading shows of their time. Perhaps you remember some of them: "Perry Mason," "Have Gun Will Travel," "The Red Skelton Show," "The Johnny Carson Show," "Rawhide," and "Outer Limits."

There are few legitimate industries that play for higher stakes than this business of broadcasting, and the mood swings that accompany the business are equally high. So periodically you think to yourself: "I gotta get away from this . . . I gotta take a clean breath . . . I gotta . . . "

Well, I did. About twenty years ago, I was approached by James Cleary, president of California State University, Northridge. He asked me if I would introduce a screenwriting emphasis at the university. Flattered, I accepted a full professorship and put my television career on hold. I would return to it, I thought, after a year or two at the most.

It didn't work out that way.

Somehow, without my noticing it, teaching became my career. At the end of the fifth year, my first class of thirteen had become ten sections with more than two hundred registered students. By the end of my tenth year, after I introduced two more advanced courses, more than three hundred undergraduates were being registered in my classes yearly.

Also at that time I was fortunate to persuade sixteen friends who were professional writers in television and film to become part-time instructors at the university. One of them came to me and said, "Why don't we have an advanced course in adaptation? At least we'll know that the student is working on a good story." He reminded me of a conversation that I had years before, while I was producing "Rawhide."

It happened during a break in my schedule. I had gone to Madrid with Clint Eastwood to make a spaghetti Western called "A Fistful of Dollars." One night the director, Sergio Leone, asked me to join him for dinner.

In the course of conversation, he began to talk about a scene that was troubling him. Somehow, I managed to contribute a notion that helped to solve his problem.

He looked at me warmly and said, "Bisogna averre gli ingeniere bravi per corregere i stupidaggini delli architetti."

Obviously it was an Italian apothegm. When I asked him what it meant, he said: "One must have smart engineers to correct the stupid mistakes of the architects." And it was in the recollection of that remark that I realized the advantage of adaptation as a learning process in the art of screenwriting.

It is well known that our method of teaching screenwriting is basically architectural. We start out by designating the building blocks of the screenplay: how it is put together. After that, in order to demonstrate how a screenplay, or the engineering, works, we ask the student to create an original story and characters, and we apply them to the building blocks.

But, as often as not, the story supplied by the student is rather frail and doesn't create opportunities to fully exploit dimensions of screenwriting. As a result, we end up with a product that may be dramatic but is unsatisfactory as a completely structured play.

In this connection, writers use two sentences constantly to signify their approval or disapproval of scripts or any parts of them. The sentences are: "It works" and "It doesn't work." When writers use those sentences, they're talking about the engineering of a script.

Hence, any discussion of the engineering factor must be inevitably diminished if the original material created by the student doesn't work. It is tantamount to teaching someone how to assemble a well-designed automobile by using parts that the student has created. If any of the parts don't work, the learning process has to be significantly undermined. Why not, then, apply the engineering process to a Rolls Royce—a story with a rich theme and characters of depth and dimension—instead of to a Model T Ford?

Think of it this way. Last year, 27,000 scripts and outlines were registered at the Writers Guild of America. Only a small percentage meet the most basic standard for judging a script: the writer has created an interesting story with dimensional characters. A published novel has already passed that test.

Another aspect of adaptation vehemently suggests itself at this point. That is the fact that year after year, as many as four out of five Academy Award nominations are adaptations. And invariably they are the winners. Moreover, this has been true throughout the history of motion pictures, from the period of the Hemingway classics, to *Dr. Zhivago* and *The Godfather*, right up to *Driving Miss Daisy* and *The Silence of the Lambs*.

But apart from that, and at the heart of the matter, I strongly believe that quality in screenwriting can be elusive and that the learning process is greatly advantaged by the energy and passion that a good story and rich characters can inspire.

Incidentally, I occasionally refer to the screenplay simply as a *play*. A screenplay is, in truth, a different product insofar as it uses a camera instead of a stage. But, in the final analysis, the play and the screenplay have the same spine. Together they share a very old and very honorable heritage as a single art form. I often use the word *play* to maintain that distinction. Nor does this change the theory upon which this book is based, namely, that an adaptation is an *original screenplay* and, as such, is the sole property of the screenwriter.

ACKNOWLEDGMENTS

My deepest appreciation goes to Theresa J. May, sponsoring editor, for her gracious and valuable assistance in bringing this work to fruition. I am especially indebted to her for availing me of the skill and attention of my copyeditor, Vicki Woodruff.

Part I

PRINCIPLES OF ADAPTATION FOR FILM AND TELEVISION

Books and films are separate art forms and it's useless to wish that one would perform the other's high-wire act. But when all's right with the heavens, movies that grow from books seem to have an extra layer of subtlety and resonance. When you see one that has, stop for a minute to think about the work of the adaptor, an artist working with respect, compassion, wit, humanity and the sharpest razor this side of Sweeney Todd.

—Sheila Benson, *Los Angeles Times* Film Critic, 1981–1991

One

INTRODUCTION

The art of screenwriting may be learned in two ways. The first and most widely employed method is by studying the structure of drama. In such a case, the student is obliged to create original characters and place them in an original story situation.

In adaptation—the second method of instruction—the student's selected source material provides not only the characters but also the story. In both writing an original story and adapting another writer's story, the learning process derives from the exercise of *writing* as it is applied to the framework of established theories of dramatic art.

An adaptation in film and television is usually based upon a novel, novelette, or short story. (Another possibility for adaptation is opera, but music is not a part of this study.)

A writer may also adapt a stage play but the process of learning is limited in such an endeavor. Since the same dramatic structure applies to both forms, the film or television adaptation of a stage play becomes chiefly a matter of opening up the story to the dimensions that are offered by the camera. Obviously, this leaves the student with much to learn about the dramatic techniques used in the adaptation of a novel.

Short stories, also, are not recommended for the student because the yarns are often spun in the first person, presenting special challenges for the novice. In other words, a short story is told through the central character's innermost thoughts. In dramatic terms, the story is *internalized*.

Internalization cannot be tolerated in drama. The only way a playwright can reveal a character's thoughts is through the use of dialogue, action, and images: that is, by what the people in the story *say* and *do*, and by what the audience is given to *see*. Only in that way can a writer communicate to the audience what is going on in a character's mind. Hence, the burden of inventing such a succession of scenes and dialogue as may be necessary to translate a complete short story into action may become a less than profitable task for the singular purpose of studying the adaptation process. However, the accomplished writer can find countless short stories that are well worth the effort of adaptation.

A novel is a narrative portrayal of fictitious characters in a series of scenes, action, and dialogue. A novel's story may be told from the viewpoint of an observer, who may or may not be the author, or it may be told in the first person by one of the characters in the story. In either case, the important point is that a *story* is *told* to the reader.

ACQUIRING RIGHTS

Before a writer begins the enormous creative effort of adapting a work, he or she should consider the legalities involved.

If a story of any kind has been published, the ownership almost certainly rests with either the original author or the publisher by virtue of a copyright, express or implied. Some material may exist in the public domain—meaning it is free to be used by others—but this copyright status should not be taken for granted.

If you are interested in and plan to adapt the work of another for financial profit, you should investigate the conditions under which you are able to use such material. Other than those works that are in public domain, you must reach some agreement with the holder of the rights before any use may take place which involves the sale of your adaptation. (No one, of course, can prevent you from adapting any material whatever, with or without approval, if it is solely for your private use as an exercise in screenwriting.)

Although an adaptation has been described as a dramatic translation of the elements of a novel, this does not mean that the adapter, or screenwriter, is required to reproduce a faithful translation of the book.

Assuming the adapter has the rights, he or she is permitted to employ any changes, alterations, or innovations in the process. Indeed, the screenwriter may even decide to use no more than the basic idea of a novel. If so, the screen credits might read: "Based upon the novel," "As suggested by the novel," or "Freely adapted from the novel." The dramatist's sole purpose is to use the story to its best advantage as a play.

This principle also apples to an individual who is adapting his or her own novel, as well as to one who is adapting the property of another. The only difference is that whereas the author of a novel, published or otherwise, probably already holds the copyright to that property, a person who undertakes to adapt and sell the property of another must first acquire its rights in order to do so. Nonetheless, it should be understood that the adapter who has secured the necessary permissions is the sole owner of any and all rights to the *adaptation*.

Hence, unless you are adapting a work solely as an exercise, such as my students do at the university (which, in my view, is the most insightful and useful method of learning the basic elements of drama and dramatic writing), you should first investigate your acquisition of the rights to the novel you have chosen to adapt.

In this regard, a simple letter of inquiry to the Copyright Office of the Library of Congress, in Washington, D.C., is the most reliable first step to take in determining who, if anyone, presently owns the rights to the work. A reply from the Copyright office includes information on the facts any writer should know about copyrights.

Since we are going to translate step by step the novel *Claire Serrat* into the screenplay *Claire Serrat*, let me tell you exactly what I did to acquire the rights to adapt and sell this screenplay.

To begin with, a novel, like any other merchandise, has a market value. Certainly I didn't look for a book on a best-seller list. My requirements were simple: the novel had to inspire me and at the same time cost little or nothing to acquire.

I wrote to the Copyright Office to inquire about the book's status. The reply stated: "*Claire Serrat*; by Ida Alexa Ross Wylie. Registered in the name of I.A.R. Wylie under 377000 following publication February 2, 1959. Renewed under RE 340-292, May 27, 1987, by Medical College of Pennsylvania, as executor."

Clearly my author was deceased; her estate owned the rights.

I wrote to the Medical College of Pennsylvania and explained my interest and purpose. I then received a letter from the college's president expressing interest in a license for *Claire Serrat* to be used in a book. According to the correspondence, the license terms would include payment of an initial fee of $500 to the Medical College of Pennsylvania as advance payment against a license fee of 10 percent of any royalties received on the *Claire Serrat* derivative works developed by myself. With that, we struck a deal.

Certainly every situation will vary, but what I am suggesting is that you attempt to get an option for a reasonable length of time in which to write and sell the screenplay. An option is an agreement that entitles the writer of the screenplay to offer it for sale under the terms and conditions agreed to by the holder of the rights, and exists for a length of time that is agreed upon by the parties involved. An option might be for three to six months, for example, and offer the possibility of renewals. Bear in mind, the deal may involve more or less difficulty in bargaining, but your expertise as a writer may prove to be the most promising asset for a book that is lying fallow. Of course, your agent, if you have one or can acquire one in the process, will understand all that.

One way or another, only a relatively small part of the novel is usable for its translation into a play. A novel, whether it is a hundred pages or a thousand, could take five to ten times longer to tell in its linear progression than would the screenplay, which compresses time and reorders events for a different dramatic effect. One paragraph in a novel could include a variety of scenes and characters that could take ten or more pages to dramatize.

This means that your book, whatever its length, must be greatly compressed in order to meet the time limits of a screenplay, customarily from ninety minutes to two hours, more or less. Although not all pages in a screenplay move at the same pace, your script should be roughly 100 to 140 pages.

Accordingly, an immediate, unconditional need exists to reduce the novel and eliminate entire scenes, characters, and subplots to the extent that the full meaning and impact of the novel can emerge without them. In order to reduce the novel to a play, the writer must revise the plot. This is another way of saying that the writer must isolate the *struggle* that will involve the *protagonist*.

To that end, a fully developed *treatment* is the foundation we will need to give our story a central dramatic purpose, or, in other words, the necessary organic structure. And so we must first find that place in the novel that is commonly described as the *point of departure* in the play. That, in dramatic language, is the point at which the protagonist is *motivated* to resolve the *issue of conflict*. (All of these italicized words will receive special attention as we proceed.)

THE NOVEL VERSUS THE PLAY

A novel is a story about people who are involved in a set of circumstances that presumably took place sometime in the past. This is true even though the author may tell the story in the present tense. Even a story about the future (science fiction, for example) is told as if the events have already taken place. A play, however, proceeds on the supposition that the story is taking place now—before your very eyes—even though the time in which the play is set may be ancient history or the distant future.

In short, a novel is a recounting; a play is a re-creation.

When you consider the novel as a form of entertainment, the author properly expects you, the reader, to make a contribution. That is, you are expected to use your imagination. In other words, you *pretend* that what you are reading is happening now. And you willingly accept that bargain in anticipation of the pleasure you expect to receive.

Unfortunately the playwright doesn't have this advantage. Since the play presents the story as if it is actually happening, it necessarily rejects the viewer's imagination. Unless you are hallucinating, you do not imagine what you see. And if an audience cannot be prevailed upon to imagine what is taking place, it follows that the dramatist cannot ask it to pretend. Although the play, like the novel, may be equally fictitious, the viewer, unlike the reader, is not imagining what he or she sees and therefore must accept what is seen as being real. In other words, the play ventures beyond the viewer's imagination: *it does not pretend; it presumes to be real.*

You read a novel patiently with the assumption that the people you are meeting will become interesting for one reason or another. You know and expect that something of a momentous nature is going to happen presently, so you willingly read on. If the author is skillful, you learn about the characters' backgrounds—where they live, what they do, and what they shouldn't do—as well as many things about their characters, such as the way you suspect they might act in certain circumstances, circumstances which you believe will happen eventually.

In most cases, the novel progresses chronologically until somebody in the story emerges with a problem. Looking back, we realize that, while reading, we have taken several left and right turns that actually had nothing to do with the protagonist's problem. But reading the novel was fun; it was what we paid for when we bought the book; after all, we agreed to use our imagination. But not so in dramaturgy. The *play* is real. *Real.* In drama, *reality is the name of the game.* What you see on the screen is what you get . . . it's not a promise, it's a *happening.* And you are there.

To be sure, the play makes the same promise of providing entertainment to the viewer, just as the novel does to the reader, but if the play is to be accepted by the audience, it must convey the impression that what is happening is *actually taking place* right before the viewers' eyes. From the very beginning of the play, they must be made to feel that what they are seeing on the screen is *real.*

A classic statement in playwriting holds that a play must be written in such a way as to condition the audience willingly to suspend its disbelief that what is taking place is real. Obviously, making an audience suspend its disbelief is nothing short of magic. Certainly, the viewers are not going to do it upon request. No. The writer must use the technique (in other words, a dramatic structure) of *involving* the viewers with the central character. Or, more precisely, the writer must get the viewers to feel that they *are* the central character.

Let us take a few minutes to examine what lies behind this sleight of hand.

A teleplay or screenplay is nothing if it is not performed. You can read a play, and many people do, but finding readers is not the primary intention of the playwright. The purpose of a play is to come alive on a stage or screen in front of an audience. Even though reading a play has its rewards, an audience would rather see it. The reason, we presume, is that seeing the play adds another dimension of dramatic art, the performance, which is probably more scintillating than the solitary experience of reading it.

If we are to understand why untold millions of viewers are daily willing to spend untold billions of dollars to sit and watch and listen to television and theatrical productions, we must explore that part of our minds in which most of our basic needs originate.

THE UNCONSCIOUS MIND

We know some predictable things about the nature of human beings. We quickly learn the difference between what is permissible and impermissible. In our infancy, we want to move, but hands restrain us. Sometimes this restraint is accompanied by an unpleasant sensation. We reach out to touch, to feel, but things are taken away. We are weaned on words like *no*, *naughty*, and *shame*.

Adolescence follows, and we experience personal rejection. All of these disappointments and rejections and failures leave us with a sense of guilt. And since we can do nothing about this mounting guilt, we grow frustrated.

Up to a point, we are able to deal with frustration. But, finally, our guilt and frustration are too much of a load to carry. So we repress them. If we did not have this ability to repress guilt, life in a restricted social order would become intolerable.

Hence, we release the pressure of our frustrations by means of a psychological device called *adjustment*. We stop feeling guilty and "forget" our pain and what caused it.

But have we forgotten? Consciously, yes. But unconsciously, no. The guilt is alive; it is simply dormant in the backs of our minds. And it wreaks havoc.

When we repress our guilt we experience conscious feelings of relief. But unconsciously, a vague unhappiness—an anguish, even—asserts itself in the form of a silent inner wish to get rid of the hateful frustrations. And we fulfill this wish by means of a mechanism called *fantasy*. Through fantasy, we repair the pain of our guilt by re-experiencing it in more pleasing ways, with endings that are more desirable. Happy endings.

Our subconscious mind asserts itself on moral issues such as right and wrong, good and bad, fair and unfair, just and unjust, decent and indecent. And we, in turn, seek to repair the pain of this guilt by fantasizing some kind of adjustment, some reconciliation, restoring our self-esteem so that we gain acceptance or seek revenge. These deriding forces in each of us seek constantly to come to terms with life.

This is the nature of our audience. When viewers attend the theater or watch a television show, it is for the purpose of being entertained by a story about the experience of others. But, in actuality, they have come to fantasize, to play the game of releasing their imprisoned emotions—their unconscious guilt. And only because they must disguise the truth of that fact—the fact that they are watching the play to get rid of their guilt—do they regard the play as mere entertainment. But subconsciously they are secretly seeking to accept the story as their own by identifying themselves with the problems of the characters in the play. This secret acceptance of the central character's struggle as the viewer's own is the key to the reality of drama.

A play is a palliative that a dramatist administers to an audience for the express purpose of relieving unconscious guilt. In these circumstances, a play is seen by an audience on two levels: the cognitive (thinking) and the unconscious (feeling). Consciously, a viewer accepts the story as someone else's (mere entertainment). But the unconscious mind secretly accepts the central character's struggle as its own. It does this by feeling sorry—sympathy—or by identification—empathy. That is why a dramatic story must contain a struggle by the protagonist to resolve a problem.

This accounts for what is often described as the *rooting interest* of the audience. It is the viewers' desire to see the struggle come out fairly, righteously, and, to their minds, decently in the end. That is the basic reason why stories about detectives and lawyers who seek justice are so popular. These characters are fighting for the common decency that most people applaud.

What we are saying is that the thrust of a play is composed of a sequence of emotional charges that begins when our curiosity is aroused by a character who becomes enmeshed in a problem and who develops a *need* to solve that problem. When he or she generates our sympathy, empathy, or antipathy—the factors that determine our rooting interest in the resolution of that problem—we are emotionally *involved* in the play. And the sooner we get involved, the better the play.

That sort of involvement does not happen that way in the novel form. Indeed, the protagonists in novels have their full share of problems, but they don't usually emerge until we have been formally introduced and have some idea of the protagonists' values and a sense of who they are, what they do, and the fabric of their surface relationships. This material concerning the central character, when properly used, provides for the playwright what we call the *backstory*. We shall explore more about that in Chapters 3 and 5.

CHOOSING THE NOVEL

The choice of a novel is, naturally, left to the adapter. This decision should not be a trivial choice or a passing fancy. If the adapter is not significantly and measurably moved by the novel, for whatever reason, the play will suffer accordingly.

When a writer undertakes an adaptation with no more than a passing desire to use it as an experiment for translating a novel into a screenplay, the likelihood is that the audience will react equally modestly, pragmatically, and unemotionally to the choice of such a story.

If screenwriting has any justification as an art form, it is fundamental that a good play must have meaning. And, to that end, the degree of a play's effectiveness will depend largely upon the richness of that meaning.

When we consider the meaning of a play, we think about the final effect felt by the audience when the play is over. In other words, the audience extracts the original purpose from the play—its *message, subtext,* or *theme.* And if the playwright can extract the subtext or theme from the novel, he or she may use it effectively in the play to significant advantage.

A VIABLE DRAMA

Some stories seem to be dramatic but are not adaptable to the play form; they are not "playable." When people in the trade refer to such a story, they say, "It doesn't work."

A story that supports a play must contain at least one central character whose emotions are being tried. In other words, dramatic stories are initiated by circumstances that cause characters to *react.* This *reaction* to a situation motivates the dramatic *action* that is the *premise* of the play.

No matter how artistically or brilliantly a story is told, if it does not present an emotional challenge for the central character or characters it is not dramatically viable. For this reason we must dispense with stories that appeal only to the intellect, such as stories that involve the explanation of lofty themes, obscure principles, or pure debate. Don't confuse the word *debate* with *contest.* A debate is purely intellectual; a contest is emotional. We do not react emotionally to intellectual issues; we may think about them, but we do not feel them.

Hence, a dramatically viable story is one that contains a character or characters who can *feel, react,* and *act* in circumstances where emotions are being tested.

More explicitly, if we ask the question, "What is the core of a dramatically viable story?", we have to say it emerges when something happens which appears to challenge a person's existence and creates in that person an immediate and unrelenting need to resolve the problem.

In dramatic language, this need is the *issue of conflict* around which the play revolves. The play is resolved only when the protagonist finally comes to terms with the issue.

THE ENGINE OF A PLAY

The engine of a play functions very much like a steam engine—but not, mind you, a locomotive. A locomotive is a vehicle. What we are talking about is the steam which is the power that moves the vehicle.

In this sense, our locomotive, or the vehicle, is the play. And, just as the locomotive's engine, or source of power, is the compressed steam, the play's engine, or source of power, is the protagonist's *problem*.

In the locomotive, power is generated by the force of the steam under pressure. The steam's freedom is opposed by its confinement. The force of the steam as it seeks to be released powers the locomotive. If the steam were freed of its confinement, the locomotive would come to a stop.

In like manner, the engine of the play is an issue generated by a force that draws its energy from some opposing force. More discretely, a play is a problem that is activated by the force of a protagonist under pressure. That is, the protagonist's freedom to function is opposed by the confining influence of the antagonist. If the protagonist were freed of the problem, the play would come to a stop.

Hence, the opposing force has the effect of moving the play forward by depriving the protagonist of the ability to go on with life until the issue of conflict is resolved. When that happens—and only then—the protagonist has come to terms with the problem, the engine stops, and the play is over.

THE ISSUE OF CONFLICT

At issue with the protagonist's objective of reaching a goal, or a final decision, is an *opposing force*, or an *antagonist*. We call this force the issue of conflict.

An issue of conflict falls into one of three categories:

1. A human force: Person versus Person.
2. A nonhuman force: Person versus Nature (or a physical obstacle).
3. An inner force: Person versus Self.

These categories describe the architectural foundation upon which all plays are constructed.

Thus, the power of a play in the first category will be generated by the force of a character who opposes the protagonist. In the second, it is a natural force or physical obstacle that opposes the protagonist; in the third, it is the protagonist's own inner force or conscience that generates the power of the play.

SIGNIFICANCE OF THE ISSUE OF CONFLICT

Conflict, then, is the fuel and the mission of drama. It increases or diminishes in direct proportion to the degree of significance your protagonist gives to the issue of conflict. Hence, the crucial issue, the objective of the play, is the significant issue of conflict. This is normally found in one of these categories:

1. Life or death.
2. Freedom or captivity.
3. Honor or degradation.
4. Health or illness.
5. Faithfulness or unfaithfulness.
6. Success or failure.

Once you have identified for yourself the plight of the protagonist in your novel as well as the significant issue of conflict as it falls into one of the above categories, you will have determined the point of departure (the opening), as well as the climax (the end), of your play.

THE WILL TO STRUGGLE

Jeremy Bentham, the ethical philosopher, thought that every human act and decision was motivated by some calculation of pleasure and pain. But the strength of this motivation depends upon the importance of the decision, which can be limited or extreme. That is, a matter which is of passing importance will be far less forcefully motivated than a life-and-death issue.

Therefore, if a person is not seriously concerned about a problem, in dramatic terms he or she doesn't truly have a problem. And the less a character cares about a problem, the less the audience cares about the problem. Why should the audience care if the character doesn't?

A characteristic of human nature is that we are inclined to dwell selfishly on our own concerns, except for the times when we are distracted by matters of more compelling interest. Therefore, the range of our interest in a distraction depends upon its seriousness. As soon as someone else's trouble becomes less compelling than our own, we return to our private thoughts.

To insure against this possibility, the issue of conflict for your protagonist must be of transcending importance, or larger than life. In most novels, the protagonist's problem is central to some socially acceptable principle or ideal with which the audience identifies. For them, the force that unconsciously drives the protagonist has an undercurrent of right or wrong, good or bad. Therefore, the significance of the conflict should be as crucial as destruction of that principle or ideal. To settle for anything less than right or good would be to compromise; to compromise would weaken the protagonist's will to struggle. Conversely, the more intensely significant the issue of conflict is for your protagonist, the more deeply it will be felt by the audience.

Two

THE TRANSITION

SUMMARIZING YOUR NOVEL

The object of the *transition* is to gain important insights in our first step, which is to reduce the size of the book to the size of the play. After you have carefully selected and read your novel at least twice, write a detailed summary describing all of the narrative developments that take place from the chronological beginning to the end of the story. When completed, the summary should contain the answers to the following questions:

Q. Who is the central character (the *protagonist*)?
Q. What is the central character's plight (the *problem*)?
Q. Who or what is the opposing force (the *antagonist*)?
Q. What is the center of the play? (The protagonist's *need* or *motivation* is the center of the play.)
Q. What is the *focus* of the play? (The protagonist's *objective* or *goal* is the focus of the play.)
Q. When did the protagonist find himself or herself in an unacceptable situation?
Q. What initiated this unacceptable situation (the backstory)?
Q. What is the issue of conflict? (Some classic conflicts are Person versus Person, Person versus Nature or some physical obstacle, and Person versus Self.)
Q. What is the significant (crucial) issue of conflict?
Q. What is the theme? (We will discuss this later.)

Note: We have already selected the novel *Claire Serrat* for adaptation, which will serve as your example as you approach each step in the development of your final screenplay.

SUMMARY

Claire Serrat

by I.A.R. Wylie

Locale: England and Provence, France

Time: The year 1948

Once a perfect young lady, now feverish and alone, CLAIRE SERRAT rested in a tousled bed in a cheap Provençal hotel with no strength or will to leave. The fact is she had no-where to go, very little money, and even less time, since she had been told by the best authority that she was soon going to die. Claire reflected on the whole messy business with detachment but no sadness or self-pity, despite the fact that she was only 25 years old.

Only a few weeks ago, though it seemed a lifetime, she had visited the English village which bore her family name and consulted the man who had brought her into the world, DR. JOHN FENWICK. He had confirmed what the Harley Street bigwigs had already told her, that she would soon die of tuberculosis. "Why do you come to me?" he asked irritably. "I'm an old, out-of-date country doctor who drinks too much. And you are obviously trying to kill yourself. Why? Why? You were such a charming child. You come of fine stock. In spite of everything, you have more than most of us to live for."

How could she have answered him? What was left of her life? She had been reared in a world which no longer ex-isted. Her father had died in the fire he had set to burn their ancestral home when he could no longer keep it up after the war. Her brother EVERETT had already given his life to the war. It was after his death that her seemingly invin-cible parents had begun to disintegrate. While Claire was at a finishing school in Switzerland, the fire had taken her home, and a letter of farewell had arrived from her mother, bidding her to put down new roots, build a new life, find a new home. Then her mother had committed suicide.

Claire returned to England, then of age. After a time, she received a thousand pounds and a few valuable pieces of furniture from her mother's estate. With these she moved into a misshapen room on the ground floor of a back-street London house. Her family's friends were dead, had fled, or had turned against her. Alone and lonely that cold November, she took to her bed, moving only when necessary. Not until ROBERT ALLWYN's imperative knock sounded at her door, bidding her join him and CANDY, did she begin to come alive again. Robert was an elegant, ambitious, handsome creature who had no doubts at all that he was destined for stardom in the theater, and who required an audience day and night. Claire inherited him that night from Candy, who happily gave him up to marry a dentist. Robert asked Claire what she could do. When he learned that she danced well and spoke French and German, he set about at once getting her a part in the play in which he was understudying the star, who drank too much. Robert plotted to get the star too drunk to go on stage opening night so that he as understudy could step into the part. By the time this was accomplished, Claire had drifted into a relationship with him from which she could not withdraw.

Their affair was stormy, but it continued, draining more and more of Claire's fragile health. Robert lived hard and restlessly, slackening his pace for no one. When Claire lay totally exhausted from his sexual excesses, he thought she had passed out from ecstasy. She hid from him the blood spots that began to appear on her handkerchief, and he requested that she try to stop her bad habit of coughing. She hated the hectic, superficial life he led, but she loved him, and she felt she was failing him. But when the doctor delivered his prognosis and Robert suggested that they marry so that she could accompany him to New York where further triumphs awaited him, she refused. "Be sure to divorce me as soon as we're there," he had said, "so that we can live happily ever after together." No, she wasn't having any of that, thank you. Better death than that, much better.

After her visit with Dr. Fenwick, she had returned to London, sold her belongings, and set out at once for France. She felt impelled to get beyond Robert's reach before he could charm her back to him. She traveled to a shabby hotel near a ghost village in Provence. At the hotel she heard some artists and a northern intellectual discussing the possible restoration of the old village with its half-ruined castle and the fine frescoes in the chapel. It was said that only one inhabitant was left, a half-mad peasant who refused to leave the remains of his ancestors. Perhaps something could be done for this village, they speculated.

Having rested at the shabby hotel, reliving her life in memory, and finding still no reason to prolong the meaninglessness of her existence, Claire paid her bill one morning, got into her two-seater, pressed the accelerator hard, and drove into the country. At last, where the road pitched abruptly downward, she crashed through a frail wooden barrier beyond which a bridge had once been. She flew upward and outward crying, "Robert!"

MARTIN THIBAUT, seeing what had happened, plunged down into the wild, tangled pit, working savagely to reach the young woman who was a tattered thing of flesh and bone and blood, trapped within the jaws of mangled steel. Thus it was that Claire awoke not to death but to the tender ministrations of a hulking stranger, a peasant who believed that his Maman, though buried in the grave, still lived and advised him to care for Claire, to save her life.

But Claire did not want to live. Yet Martin still cared for her with stolid patience as though she were one of his lambs, feeding her goat's milk and washing her daily, for she was utterly helpless even as she grew stronger against her will. Gradually she realized that she would be paralyzed from her waist down.

Through the long summer months the tender, strong, handsome Martin cared for her, while she struggled against her hatred for the one who kept her alive against her will and brought her back to the life which meant nothing to her. Little by little Robert became no more than an aching memory. Her fragility disappeared and curves appeared, muscles developed under Martin's careful massage. He told her of his life, how the village had been deserted during the war, with no one left but his mother who had waited for him to return. He had come back, wounded and out of his mind, but his mother had cared for him like a child; then it had been his turn to care for her when she lay dying. Now she was in the grave but not really gone, for she had promised never to leave him.

Claire was afraid of this strange man who cared for her, whom she felt would never let her go. Yet, though they slept in the same big bed, he never touched her. How long could it last? She had even more reason to fear him: he had confessed to her that he had killed a woman he loved, a city woman, beautiful like herself.

Then in a storm, Claire suddenly discovered that she could walk. Secretly she exercised and planned to escape when Martin went on one of his infrequent trips for supplies. But when she laboriously ventured out, she met him on the road. He had come back to tell her some men were coming from the town: he wanted to warn her, for her passport had expired. He had shaved his beard and wore a white shirt to please her—when he saw her walking, great racking sobs burst from him. She took him in her arms, comforting him, and all her hatred dissolved.

The men who arrived were the artists and the intellectual who had plans to restore the village. They spoke of their plans to Martin, who looked steadily away when they turned to Claire and asked if she, too, belonged in Provence. Martin knew she had planned to run away from him. But Claire then remembered how her mother had told her to put down new roots, to make a new home.

She and Martin were alike in their losses. Together they could build something new and good. So Claire smiled at the men and said, "Yes, I belong here, too."

SUBTEXT

The subtext of a story is the briefest possible synopsis of the subject, the object, and the conclusion of the story. After you have given the summary your careful consideration, write the subtext of your novel.

Claire Serrat

Subtext

A fragile, lovely young woman, who is one of the last of a dying class—the English aristocracy—is thrown out on her own when she loses her parents and ancestral home to death and fire. Falling in love with an ambitious, rising actor, she sticks with him until her health is ruined. When she tries to end her life near a deserted French village, she is saved by a half-mad peasant, handsome and strong, who regains his own sanity by nursing her back to health. Each having a new wish to live for the other, they plan a new life at last.

After you have written the subtext, consider the following questions and answers.

Q. Why was I asked to painstakingly reduce the story to its subtext?
A. To see at the earliest stage how I might later reduce the novel to its more restricted dimensions as a play.

Having established that, let us now answer the questions that were earlier proposed:

Q. Who is the central character?
A. The protagonist is Claire Serrat.
Q. What is the protagonist's plight?
A. She finds herself in a deserted village with a madman.
Q. Who or what is the opposing force?
A. Martin Thibaut is the antagonist.
Q. What is the center of the play? (The protagonist's *need* or *motivation* is the center.)
A. Claire must free herself from Martin.
Q. What is the focus of the play? (The protagonist's *objective* or *goal* is the focus.)
A. Claire must try to get out alive.
Q. When did the protagonist find herself in this unacceptable situation?
A. Claire encountered Martin after her attempted suicide.
Q. What initiated this unacceptable situation?
A. All of the circumstances in the book that led up to Claire's present problem initiated the unacceptable situation. This is the backstory—the events that took place in the book before our play opens.
Q. What is the issue of conflict?
A. The story's conflict is woman versus man.
Q. What is the significant or crucial issue of conflict?
A. Claire's conflict is freedom or captivity.
Q. What is the theme?
A. To be needed is the supreme fulfillment of life.

THEME

There are many reasons why individuals opt for writing as a career. But whatever the motive, sincere or spurious, the urge to write is basically an urge to be heard: to be able to say something that *means* something. So, let us stop for a moment and consider: why do we fancy our choice of story? What is the point of it?

When we consider the meaning of a play, we are referring to the conclusion that is reached or the message that is extracted by the audience. This meaning is called the theme.

At the outset, let us clear up a widely held misconception regarding the usefulness of a message in a play. The notion was given credence when it was attributed to the late, celebrated Samuel Goldwyn.

Addressing a writer who had improperly used his theme, Goldwyn fumed: "I have an agreement with Western Union; they don't make movies, and I don't send messages."

Goldwyn's exasperation grew out of the fact that the writer had mistakenly articulated the theme of his screenplay by putting it into the dialogue of his characters. In such a case, it is indeed more advisable to turn the message over to Western Union.

In short, a theme is something that is felt by the audience after it has thought about the protagonist's problem as it was resolved in the play. Any mention of the theme by any of the characters in the play before the resolution of the problem will have the effect of defeating the play's essential purpose. Resolution is the key to the play's meaning; its meaning is its theme.

Consequently, if the lasting imprint or a play—or the quality that makes a play memorable—is activated for an audience by the theme, we should consider how the writer postulates the theme and how the writer benefits from adapting a work.

THEME AS A MECHANISM

The primary purpose of a theme is to shed or add new light to the common experience of humankind. This is achieved when the audience reconsiders its conclusions after experiencing the play. This understanding of the substance of the problem avails an audience of a deep satisfaction—a sense of reconciliation, acceptance, repairing of self-esteem, or fulfillment. That is its value to the audience.

From the writer's point of view, however, a theme can have an additional positive influence on the construction of the play. Extracting the theme from the story before writing the play can enable the writer to eliminate material that is not related to the problem.

An adaptation is more effective than an original play for students studying dramatic structure because the subject of theme can be so effectively explored. The writer of an original drama may not know what the meaning is until the play is finished, unless he or she designs the play for the express purpose of conveying a message or theme.

The advantage to the adapter of knowing the theme of the novel in advance of writing the play can be an invaluable aid in helping to eliminate from the play any material that does not relate to the message (i.e., the protagonist's problem).

One of the more difficult decisions in an adaptation, especially for those who are undertaking this task for the first time, lies in establishing the dramatic parameters of the play: in other words, excluding those excursions in the novel that do not contribute to the ultimate resolution of the protagonist's problem. Conversely, knowing the theme of the play helps to restrict the plot of the play to only those scenes that are integral to its meaning.

A play can mean different things to different people. Generally, one concept will emerge with enough prominence to dominate. To this extent, the adapter's opportunity to discern the theme of the novel before plotting the play is a considerable asset.

The theme of a play can be told in a word, a phrase, a sentence, or more. Essentially, it is the moral of a story. For example, the theme of the entire Alfred Hitchcock mystery series was "Crime doesn't pay." More complex themes are "Civilization will flourish as long as freedom survives" and "Ruthless ambition leads to its own destruction." More simplistic themes are "Love conquers all" and "Hell hath no fury like a woman scorned." Sometimes the theme of a play may be elusive, but the adapter should try to find it.

In order to extract the theme, or meaning, of the novel, a single reading may suffice. However, in planning an adaptation, you must acquire a far more insightful sense and feeling, especially for the main characters—their values, traits, and mannerisms, as well as their motivations and conflicts. In short, you should acquire the same measure of familiarity with the characters—especially the central characters—as you would if you had created them originally.

After you resolve the theme or message try to find any steps in the development of the story that are alien to the theme. *Then avoid them. They do not belong in your play*. Reread the book to find them. This step will help enormously in condensing the novel.

One of the aspects that best reveals the skillfulness of a dramatist is the ability to write economically. Hence, nothing irrelevant to the theme should be found in the play.

Also, the dramatist will *repeat nothing*, either in speech or action, that has been said or done before. To this extent, your being able to discern the theme in advance is a considerable help.

However, once you extract the theme from the novel, you must be certain that you don't share it with the characters in your screenplay. For as surely as night follows day, your characters will talk about it if they get wind of the message. And, if they do, you will have fallen prey to the mischief that so disturbed Samuel Goldwyn.

The moment you place social pronouncements in the mouths of your characters, the theme will dominate the problem—your characters will be reflecting what is on your mind instead of what is on their minds. What should be on their minds is a problem, not a theme.

Remember, a theme may mean different things to different people. *Claire Serrat*'s theme is based on my own personal reaction to the story.

Three

PLOT

STRUCTURE

Every adaptation of a novel is built upon a plot that is the screenwriter's own invention. Plot is the manner in which the adapter chooses to recreate the story. As the writer approaches a problem which, in turn, creates an issue of conflict for the protagonist, he or she is well advised to follow guidelines and use dramatic directions that reinforce the sturdiness of the vehicle that is going to power the play. Thus far we have considered the essential elements that constitute the fabric of the play; now we are going to assemble what we have described as the engine.

A plot involves two aspects: (A) its architecture and (B) its engineering. We first will look at the design of the plot and after that we will examine its functions.

To create a play which will not only captivate the audience while it is being performed but also remain memorable afterward, the screenwriter may use specific techniques that will contribute to that end. The manner in which a writer exercises these techniques is the final test of his or her skill.

Plays which are the most enduring are made memorable chiefly because of the characters involved in the story. Yet those characters could hardly become memorable without the support of a well-laid plot.

We know that a story contains a sequence of events that are strung together—told, more or less, in chronological order. A plot, on the other hand, is a rearrangement of the events of a story into a pattern of organically connected parts that accomplishes the dramatic purpose of creating increasingly crucial decisions for the protagonist. In other words, the primary purpose of a good plot is to hold the unswerving attention of the audience. And the element that holds the attention of the audience may be summed up in a single word: *suspense*.

Suspense

Suspense is a dramatic contrivance by which the dramatist creates a sense of urgent anticipation about a condition which is crucial for the protagonist. The audience's anticipation grows or diminishes in direct proportion to the degree of sympathy or empathy its members feel for the protagonist's plight. Bear in mind, the audience's emotion will be governed by the measure of anxiety which the protagonist feels. In short, *the feeling of suspense in the audience will be equal to the extremes to which the protagonist is driven to defend himself or herself against the opposing force.*

The skillful dramatist successfully weaves together two forms of suspense. Major suspense is derived from the protagonist's struggle with the main problem as it continues to deteriorate. Minor suspense is derived from fragmentary incidents—serious challenges that must be met but can be resolved quickly, or moments of danger that grow out of but are not directly related to the solution of the protagonist's problem.

The foundation of drama, and therefore your plot, exists in the problem of the play. At times the play may include subplots—small, subsidiary stories that involve subordinate characters. Although there are usually good reasons for including these subplots in the story and play, their removal from the story has no serious effect upon the play. Also, if and when the subplots are needed for the sake of clarity in the telling of the story, they can be briefly integrated in the form of backstory, which is revealed in some brief references in dialogue by the characters inserted at appropriate moments in the forward development of the play, or perhaps in a flashback. (This will be discussed further later in Chapter 3.)

Beginning, Middle, and End

No matter how short or long the play may be, the plot is divided into three parts: Act I, the beginning; Act II, the middle; and Act III, the end. (In television, when the need warrants it, plays are divided into four, five, and even more segments which are captioned as acts. In truth, these are essentially artificial breaks designed simply to accommodate commercial messages. They have nothing to do with the basic dramatic structure of the three-act play.)

What's more, each of the three acts is divided into three parts. That is, Act I has a beginning, middle, and end. So do Act II and Act III. Moreover, this rule of thumb applies to any scene in the play.

In Act I, the significant issue of conflict emerges or promises to emerge. In other words, the opposing force is felt. As the act proceeds, the conflict intensifies; the problem worsens. Ultimately, the opposing force appears to be beyond control. Act I ends. The *problem* and the *issue of conflict* are joined—the beginning.

In Act II, the protagonist takes stronger measures to eliminate the conflict, but unexpected complications cause the problem to deteriorate further. Ultimately, the protagonist faces a situation of imminent failure unless extreme measures are taken. The conflict has reached a *crisis*—the middle.

In Act III, the extreme measure is taken. But instead of eliminating the conflict, the problem becomes more insoluble. A do-or-die decision has to be made. It is made, and the play has reached its *climax*. The protagonist has come to terms with the issue of conflict—the end.

Accordingly, the plot of a play arouses a growing emotional response in the audience by presenting a character who is caught up in a problem with which the audience sympathizes, empathizes, or antipathizes. The character is torn by the issue of conflict resulting from that problem. The issue continues to deteriorate until a crisis is reached. Then it is resolved in the climax.

ACTION

Three aesthetic principles of dramatic structure, incorrectly attributed to Aristotle, refer to the unities of time, place, and action. Today, with the high degree of cinematic flexibility and the freedom of movement that is afforded the television and film writer, the first two principles have lapsed into desuetude.

But the unity of action is still a necessary discipline in play writing. This means that a play must have a single main plot and must be told from a single point of view (POV). Consequently, the unity of problem and conflict is confined to the protagonist.

No matter how long or short your novel may be, whether it contains two characters or two hundred, the unity of your play based upon that story demands that it be limited to those developments—and only those developments—which reflect the POV of the protagonist as he or she attempts to deal with the problem. In short, the play is resolved from the protagonist's POV.

Choices + Decisions + Changes = Action

The *action* of a play revolves around the decisions that the protagonist is forced to make as he or she attempts to deal with the alternatives that are presented by the antagonist. These decisions grow more urgent as the *choices* become more difficult to make in the struggle to resolve the problem. Each of the protagonist's *decisions* brings with it a *change* in circumstances which, in turn, creates the need for yet another decision in the eventual outcome of the problem.

This is the process:

Something happens—the *Problem*.
Something must be done—the *Choice*.
Something is done—the *Decision*.
Something happens—the *Change*.
Something must be done—the *Choice*.
Something is done—the *Decision*.
Something happens—the *Change*.
(And so the process continues.)

Consequently, since the viewers presumably care about the protagonist—having a rooting interest in what happens—they are equally involved in the decisions.

This may be clearer if you think of the process in terms of your own daily experiences. Each of us is most relaxed when our affairs remain constant. Change is unsettling; the familiar appeals to our sense of security. At the moment we are forced to contemplate a change in our affairs, we grow uncertain—our anxiety begins to mount. This emotion is attributable to our latent fear of the unknown, a human characteristic which dramatists exploit to the fullest. If there are no choices, decisions, and changes, there is no action. Where there is no *action*, there is no emotion. Where there is no emotion, there is no involvement of the viewer. Where there is no viewer involvement, there is no play.

Culminating Events

Each step that furthers the action, namely, each step that militates for or against the protagonist, moves the story to a higher point of suspense. These culminating events move the story forward, as they relate to the problem and the conflict. As a corollary to this, any event which does not culminate in a further intensification of the clash between the problem and the conflict for the protagonist is an unwarranted excursion, or a departure from the plot, and is therefore to be avoided.

All of the other material of the novel that surrounds these culminating events, such as what happened before the problem was precipitated, what took place between scenes, or any other information that digresses and is not connected with the action involved in these culminating events, should be rigidly excluded from the treatment of the play. This means that, immediately following the establishment of the opening scenes which introduce the principal characters, the play's first culminating event should be the emergence of the problem, the choices, and the first decision.

Complications

It may be said, therefore, that the key to play writing is the art of presenting the point of view of the protagonist in a series of developing *complications*, each of which instigates a culminating event.

These culminating events are the building blocks of your play. When one event leads to the next, it is because of a further complication that has arisen which must be met by your protagonist.

Consequently, complications are the emotional glue that connects the protagonist to the audience. Since each complication has a limited well of interest, it is fair to conclude that the dramatic purpose of each new complication is to revitalize the flagging emotions of the audience.

Exposition

Every teleplay or screenplay begins with the postulation of a problem for the protagonist. Obviously, the characters are motivated by conditions and circumstances that occurred before the play started. Since these affairs are not a part of the play's main concern, they are properly excluded from the plot.

Nonetheless, what happened in the past must be made known to the audience if viewers are to understand what is happening in the present. While it is true that an audience may enjoy being mystified on occasion, the people still expect to be provided with all the facts. Never cheat an audience by withholding any of the facts. However, if information about the past does not move the play forward by presenting new and suspenseful complications, how do we manage to apprise the audience of these necessary facts without diminishing emotional involvement?

We do it by artfully weaving the orienting information into the fabric of the play so that the viewer doesn't realize it's being explained. The skilled dramatist doles out the information by masquerading it in some form of action. This can be done in several ways and should be done as early as possible, preferably in the first act.

One way of handling exposition is by means of titles: for instance, PROVENCE, 1948. A second method—to be used only on very rare occasions—is through a *narrator*. A third technique is called a *flashback*, which we will consider in a moment. Another common way is for characters to reveal information in dialogue.

Simple examples are of the character who dictates the facts to a secretary or reveals information in a telephone call. A couple of well-placed telephone calls can reveal a mass of information. But a far better way to give information is by integrating the information into scenes of high emotion—scenes that pretend to progress the story.

For example, "This is the danger you're walking into, 007," the Chief might say to James Bond. Then the Chief proceeds to fill in the audience with everything that happened before the play started, and we listen with baited breath.

In short, the best exposition conveys the feeling that all of the information which is volunteered or solicited fits into the action of the plot. Yet, this information has nothing to do with the problem or its solution. A good writer piques the curiosity of the audience so that the viewers eagerly want to know what you're telling them.

For example, if a character says, "Why do you think I had to get out of the country?" you may be sure that the audience will want to know what happened before the play started.

Briefly, if you tailor your exposition so that the person giving the information feels urged to give it and the one receiving the information is anxious to know what he or she does not yet know, you will be on safe ground.

An example of exposition at its most artful is one in which the screenplay opens as the protagonist is delivered in chains to an insane asylum. The man, who is apparently sane in every respect, seems ecstatic about being delivered there. In short order, he appears before the medical supervisor of the institution to be interviewed about his background, and we learn why he is so happy to be delivered to this institution—admittance to it was his device for getting out of jail. Perhaps you recall the picture, *One Flew Over the Cuckoo's Nest*, with Jack Nicholson as the protagonist.

An expositional device which is recommended for use with the greatest caution is called the *flashback*. It is a risky technique and, if used incorrectly, may have the adverse effect of bringing a play to an abrupt halt by playing out a whole scene that took place in the past. If, as we have said, this past information is not a part of the play's main concern, it does not advance the story. To that extent, it distracts the audience from its immediate concern with the problem, thereby robbing the play of its energy.

There are times, however, when flashbacks are not only acceptable but also appropriate, effective, and necessary, because they contribute to the forward progress of the play. More particularly, if you have a character who has a problem that is integrally related to an incident in the past and that incident motivates the character's choices, thus involving a decision about the present problem, the flashback can be extremely effective. The development of *Claire Serrat* provides examples of the flashback technique.

Violence

The spinal column of your play is action—more particularly, extremes of action. An audience wants to love or hate; they want to admire deeply or resent strongly. They are not much moved by in-between. They are, in truth, a collection of cruel inquisitors who will not compromise their tastes or their passions.

Such people have little patience for passing the time with a character who maunders through byways, one who loses sight of life-and-death struggle. They will abide such peregrinations in a novel, but not in the real life of a play. Yes, that's what plays are: real life. Plays consist of people who are constantly vulnerable, always fighting for survival in lifetimes that are endlessly arrayed with complications or, in terms of drama, *conflict*.

And dramatic conflict is the substance of violence.

Time and again, we have stressed the clash between *problem* and *conflict* in a well-made, realistic play. To believe that this can be accomplished without involving violence is to fail to understand the meaning of drama. Conflict breeds violence as certainly as mischief breeds trouble. There is no way to write effective drama without conflict's implicit violence.

Strongly opposed to this axiom, however, is gratuitous violence, or the use of violence for its own sake. It is then that the writer is resorting to false and lamentable trickery. It is human nature to be fascinated by such unwelcome abuse. But when violence is employed for the sole purpose of gratuitously stimulating our interest in the matter at hand, that is no longer the type of violence that is properly part of drama. Brutality is not art. It is merely a contrivance that signals the weakness of the play.

The violence in true drama resides not in grotesquery but in the torment of a decision to act. The suggestion of dramatic violence should make itself felt in every development of the play, usually in the suggestion of danger. Consider: a man reaches for a gun—danger and violence; a ship founders in an angry sea—danger and violence; a child clings to life at the bottom of an abandoned well—danger and violence. Danger and violence in your novel will be found in the threatening nature of choices and decisions.

The dramatist is obligated to fan the passions of the audience. The writer cannot do this without generating great and still greater dramatic conflict: in other words, crucial and more crucial decisions. But to substitute a pageant of gratuitous brutality for such dramatic action is a mark of failure.

Four

THE PREMISE

A story is the accounting of an item of interest. Be sure to underscore that word *interest*. Unless you do, you may overlook its significance.

A story that is not refreshing, intriguing, or different enough to provoke attention and interest is not worth adapting. It is like a joke that everyone has already heard. This, however, should not contradict the notion that an old story can be told in new and different ways.

If a story is to be of interest to its readers, listeners, or viewers, its purpose must be to entertain, inform, or enlighten its audience. Hence, if it communicates nothing new, it is not worthy of dramatizing.

But assuming the story fulfills the requirements of entertainment, it becomes a *dramatic* story only when and if it is endowed with a *capacity for dramatic action*: that is, the elements of a *premise*.

The dramatic action of a story is the issue of that story. It is the core, the basic concept, or the premise. Your screenplay, as you develop it, will be concerned exclusively with this premise, and will never depart from it.

Let us put the premise under the light of the following questions:

Q. What is a premise?
A. A premise is the plot of a play distilled to its essence. It might be described as the acorn of an oak tree: the seed of a dramatic story.
Q. What is a dramatic story?
A. It is a personal story of an individual or individuals with a problem.
Q. Is every story dramatic if it contains a problem?
A. No. A story is dramatic only when the problem strikes an emotional response in the individual.
Q. What is emotion?
A. Emotion is the immediate, knee-jerk state of feeling by an individual, usually an affected sense of consciousness in which joy, sorrow, fear, hate, and love are experienced.

Q. What is the test of a successful dramatic play?

A. The audience is the test. If the viewers are not concerned about the main character, the story has not reached them emotionally. The magic word is *care*. Do they *care* about what happens? Are they sympathetic?

Q. When is a plot dramatic?

A. A plot is dramatic when it contains an individual who feels a need to defend his or her values. It is this need that motivates the drama.

Q. What is drama?

A. Drama is a study of the human struggle to maintain our values. It grows out of the fact that we are all destructible. Therefore, we must constantly cope with the needs (values) that affect our survival. When one of our values is challenged, it motivates our will to destroy the opposing force.

Q. What is the substance of a premise?

A. In substance, a premise consists of three integral parts, usually no longer than a paragraph each, that contain and mark the beginning (*conflict*), middle (*crisis*), and end (*climax*) of a situation in which an individual is motivated by a need to defend values against an opposing force.

A THEORETICAL PREMISE

ACT I

The Beginning

In the course of a character's activities, an event occurs which threatens the protagonist's values (the problem). As a result, the protagonist is motivated to eliminate the opposing force. But the problem deteriorates until it becomes irreconcilably opposed to the protagonist's general welfare. The objective is established. End Act I.

Conflict

ACT II

The Middle

With renewed effort, the protagonist continues the struggle to vanquish the antagonist. However, continuing complications (crises), cause a further deterioration of the problem. Complications grow more intolerable; an imminent development threatens to be fatal. Something dramatic must be done, or all will be lost. End Act II.

Crisis

ACT III

The End

The protagonist manages to survive the crisis, and the struggle continues. Finally, with ingenuity, resourcefulness, and good fortune, the problem is resolved in a climactic scene. Win or lose, the protagonist has come to terms with his or her values. End of Act III.

Climax

Note: the dramatic definition of *conflict* is different from the word as it is used in common parlance. Conflict in drama delineates the will of an individual to defend individual values. If the will of the protagonist weakens, the play weakens; if the will is lost, the play is over.

QUESTIONING YOUR PREMISE

Given your chosen point of departure, answer the following questions as they relate to Act I of your premise. Our answers here relate to *Claire Serrat*.

Q. What problem has emerged for your protagonist?
A. Claire Serrat awakens to find herself in the presence of a half-mad peasant named Martin.
Q. What is the issue of conflict?
A. The issue of conflict is classic: woman versus man (Claire versus Martin).
Q. What is the significance of the issue of conflict?
A. Claire must fight for freedom over captivity.
Q. At what point does the issue of conflict emerge?
A. It emerges when Claire discovers that she is helplessly paralyzed.
Q. When do the problem and conflict become joined? (What brings Act I to an end?)
A. They join together when Martin makes it clear that he has no intention of letting Claire go.

Now, after you repeat this process for Act II and Act III, we will reduce our play to a three-paragraph premise.

PREMISE: CLAIRE SERRAT

ACT I

CLAIRE SERRAT, frustrated beyond her will to live, attempts to end her life by crashing her car near a deserted

French village. Failing in her suicide attempt, she awakens to find herself being attended by a half-mad French peasant, the solitary inhabitant of the village. Her legs paralyzed and unable to move, she pleads with the man to return her to her people and civilization. But her efforts appear to be in vain when he reveals that his intentions are to keep her for himself.

Conflict

ACT II

As time passes, and against Claire's will, Martin ministers to her health and her needs, including her daily ablutions. Claire's protestations are in vain; her pleas are ignored. Claire learns that Martin asks his mother for advice and receives it—but she is dead, in her grave. And, as time passes, Claire senses that Martin's feelings for her are growing stronger. How long will she be safe? Then, too, Martin confesses to her that he once killed the woman he loved—a city woman, beautiful like herself. One night, in a frightening storm, Claire sits up abruptly and realizes that her legs have responded. She can walk!

Crisis

ACT III

Secretly Claire exercises and plans to make her getaway when Martin goes on one of his infrequent trips for supplies. But when the time comes, he returns and accidentally catches her in her flight. Seizing her roughly now in his anger, he carries her back to the house, tears the clothes off of her, and forces himself on her. But, as he vents his need for her, Claire senses that he is no longer a madman but the one who has made her well and strong again, and she responds. Finally Martin admits that the village is no place for her, that she must have her freedom. And as he takes her to the highway, they meet the artists and an intellectual who had plans to restore the village. They speak to Martin about the plans; when they ask Claire if she, too, belongs in the village, she smiles and says, "Yes, I belong here, too."

Climax

If you have been afraid to condense your novel this tightly for fear of losing much of it, we should make it clear that this premise represents the action of your play reduced to its barest bones. As such, it sets forth and describes (1) a protagonist who is involved in a problem of disastrous proportions; (2) an antagonist of great strength who apparently is positioned to frustrate the protagonist; and (3) the protagonist who on the verge of defeat manages to come to terms with her values.

The premise is the tip of the iceberg: the story lies under the surface. But now, the following must be clear: whatever the genesis of your premise, it should contain two elements—(1) a character or characters, and (2) a happening, something which jeopardizes the character's well-being (or, indeed, life). By contriving to make those opposing forces clash, you are creating the substance of drama. Conversely, if one of these elements is absent, the story will not be endowed with dramatic action or feeling.

These principles apply to comedy as well as drama. If you doubt this, consider any comedy that comes to your mind. Doesn't the fun grow out of the victim's plight, which is occasioned by an opposing force?

Only after you have identified for yourself the plight of your protagonist as well as the final scene (that is, the climax), will you begin to see the straight line of your adaptation that proceeds from the emergence of the problem to the resolution of the play. Getting there is the issue of conflict.

Conflict is the fuel of drama. Its emergence and the height of its intensity are governed by the degree of significance your protagonist gives to his or her values.

In its best use, the conflict keeps the problem alive, occasionally improving but largely worsening for the protagonist as it resonates right up to the play's end. The uncertainty of that outcome is the basis of the play's *suspense*. These elements combine to work successfully provided that your audience sympathizes, empathizes, or antipathizes with your protagonist.

Five

CHARACTER

The dramatist's range and depth of investigation in exploring the characters of the novel depends largely on the kind of play being adapted and the use the writer will make of them. In melodramas, for example, where the story deals with heroic characters who are uncomplicated and mainly concerned with the convolutions of the plot as they seek to reach a goal, the dimensions of the character are, more often than not, subsumed or taken for granted.

In the mere entertainment of a play, we are all inclined to believe that a cop is a cop is a cop. The same applies to lawyers for the defense, cowboys who wear white hats, doctors who still make house calls, and so on. In such cases, the adapter shows skill by creating an intriguing manner of speech for such a stock character.

In more probative dramas, however, where the novelist has created a character who is unique, original, and complicated, the adapter may need to read the novel three or four times to understand the character and to translate that understanding into an effective character in the play.

Were it not for the fact that our author, I. A. R. Wylie, has told us a good deal about the characters, this step in the translation of the play might have been far more laborious. As matters stand, we are now in a position to depend on the book. The chronological beginning of the novel naturally provides your backstory: that is, your exposition—what happened before your play opens.

To repeat: the important choices an individual makes when faced with critical decisions are governed by his or her values and drives. These values may be reasoned (a principle, credo, or commitment), or felt (the subconscious will). In either case, the primal force of the individual's character dominates will—sometimes even against his or her own better judgment.

And so it is with us all: our lives are pledged to the order of our priorities—to fixed ideas. These values are based on some overwhelming drive: to be true to what we feel is a matter of the utmost importance—a personal and private article of faith. These values and drives can be expressed in many strong words: wealth, power, lust, honor, acclaim, love, glory, adulation, supremacy, and so on. Whatever the value may be, its possessor is driven to defend itself from—perhaps even destroy—anything or anyone who challenges it.

When our values are challenged by a threatening, opposing force, we experience an emotional conflict of anxiety. Hence, when the drives of one individual crash head-on with the desires of another, the resulting emotional *action* is described dramatically as Person versus Person. The same emotional effect comes when the adversary is a natural force or obstacle, or Person versus Nature. And, again, the most highly dramatic issue of conflict exists when an individual, having two values of equal priority which cannot coexist in the circumstances of a problem, opposes himself or herself: Person versus Self.

The screenwriter cannot impart a character's values in words as a novelist does. The values must make themselves felt through surface characteristics of behavior, conduct, and communication that indirectly express or imply a condition that others can accept. In other words, a character's values are, in the main, compatible with actions that demonstrate viewpoint, temperament, and disposition. And, since these observable characteristics tend to match the individual's values, they provide us with insight and predictability.

The observable characteristics of an individual which tend to reflect values are described as *traits*. We directly understand someone's traits by their *reactions*. While values are not readily observable, traits are highly visible. Furthermore, as the writer attempts to add aspects of personality to characters, he or she will be aware of the mannerisms in the novel that add color, style, and charm to those individuals who are richly delineated.

It is because of a character's values that the issue of conflict becomes more crucial as the play progresses. A value which has only a passing importance to an individual will be far less forcefully motivating than a life-and-death issue. Also, the more intensely significant the issue of conflict is for a protagonist, the more deeply will it be felt by an audience.

ANALYZING YOUR CHARACTERS

As an aid to establishing the background of your characters, evaluate them with this tridimensional analysis.

1. Physical characteristics: Age? Height and weight? Carriage or bearing? Appearance (neat, sloppy, pleasant, unpleasant, etc.)? Handicaps?
2. Social characteristics: Class? Race? Religion? Job? Income? Education? Family background? Skills? Marital status? Children?
3. Psychological characteristics: Ambitions, goals, and failures? Disappointments? Outlook on life (pessimistic, optimistic, angry, militant, resigned, defeatist)? Sexuality (normal, abnormal, moral, immoral)? Temperament (tranquil, nervous)? Maladjustments or disturbances? Talents? Education? Sensibility (taste, poise, style)? Sensitivity (awareness, perception)?

Make a similar list of your character's traits. When you do, bear this in mind: it is both possible and interesting for a character to have conflicting traits. It is possible to be aggressive, brash, and cowardly, or cheerful, religious, and immoral. Such contradictions lead to refreshing surprises. But once you have established a character's values and traits, they must remain constant.

The following list of basic characteristics is a useful aid in identifying traits.

dirty—immaculate
gentle—violent
clever—stupid
cheerful—morbid
humorous—humorless
dainty—sloppy
brave—cowardly
avaricious—generous
boastful—modest
cruel—kind
extravagant—miserly
simple—complex
vulgar—wholesome
obstinate—yielding
gregarious—withdrawn
fair—ruthless
moral—immoral
optimistic—pessimistic
faithful—fickle

calm—nervous
healthy—sickly
naïve—worldly
arrogant—courteous
awkward—graceful
shrewd—guileless
cunning—ingenuous
egotistic—self-effacing
hysterical—placid
snobbish—democratic
lucid—obscure
gallant—rude
garrulous—taciturn
energetic—lazy

The simplest way of establishing these traits is by considering the way the character reacts to a situation. In an emergency, for example, some people are cool, while others become agitated; one type of person will be blunt, another diplomatic; some people view trouble with optimism, others darkly; some proceed with energy and dispatch; others are phlegmatic. Thus, in an endless variety of ways, you can classify people as careless or precise, sloppy or neat, hasty or calculating—with all of these traits measured by how the individuals react to circumstances.

As you sharpen your awareness of the unique nature of the people in your play, especially as you develop the principal characters' foibles, look for a third dimension that adds color to their personalities. You might call it "seasoning" the character with the unique traits that we call style. This is to be found in a character's *mannerisms*. These are personal characteristics, such as a man who clears his throat before he talks, a woman who always gestures wildly with her hands, a child who constantly scratches his head, and so on.

The purpose of this character study is to create a climate of increasing suspense as the story unfolds. Hence, if the key to creating dramatic suspense resides in the continual deterioration of the protagonist's problem, it is important to find the character's energy to fuel your screenplay. This, then, is what your treatment will set forth in a succession of scenes from the beginning to the end of the play.

CAUSE AND EFFECT

The only acceptable procedure for telling a story in the form of a dramatic play is through a series of steps, starting with the introduction of a problem at the beginning and concluding with the resolution of the problem at the end. Each of these steps reveals how one event causes an effect that leads to the next event.

From the first step to the last, a play is a model of cause and effect. That is to say: something happens, the effect of which causes something to be done, the effect of which causes something to happen, the effect of which causes something to be done. The sequence is repeated over and over and over again. A play is an organic continuum of cause and effect.

Early on, we said that a novel tells you *what* took place; the play tells you *why*. Take the test yourself. Start with the last event of any scene or any act and ask: Why did this happen? The previous step must reflect the cause. This pattern must continue all the way back to the beginning, where the problem, which is the cause of the entire screenplay, was initiated. Consequently, if something took place before the point at which you opened your screenplay, that information has to be doled out in such a way that it does not interrupt the forward progress of the screenplay.

As we have continued to emphasize, your screenplay, unlike the novel, will begin with a problem (motivation) for the protagonist. The skilled writer introduces the problem as soon as possible. Obviously that problem didn't spring into existence out of thin air. It grew out of circumstances that led up to the problem, before your screenplay began—things the audience may need to know.

At this time, therefore, you should ask yourself: what happened in the early part of the novel, before my screenplay began, that set the stage for my protagonist's present dilemma? In other words, what did the protagonist do? What were the early circumstances that contributed to the problem?

If this information early in the novel reveals facts that the viewer needs to know in order to understand clearly what is going on, then you, the adapter, must artfully weave that information into the fabric of the screenplay. And, you must do it in such a way as not to interrupt the audience's involvement in the protagonist's growing problem. At this point you should reread the book. Another good reason to do this is to get to know the central character more intimately.

It is the character of the protagonist—the uniqueness of his or her values—that determines the direction of the play. The manner in which the events develop are, in the final analysis, governed by the actions of the central character who must make all the necessary decisions. To the extent, therefore, that the protagonist has the burden of moving the play forward, it is reasonable to conclude that the playwright must have the most intimate knowledge of the protagonist's inner being. It probably would surprise no one to learn of the enormous amount of time that professional writers apply to the business of researching the authenticity of their stories. Most people, however, would be hard-pressed to believe the inordinate expenditure of time and effort that is made to acquire the all-important depth of intimacy with the principal characters who eventually bring life to the play.

Fortunately for you, this intimate knowledge is provided by the author. You do your research through the simple act of rereading the book. So, if it is vital to know your characters in order to bring your story alive, it may be fatal if you don't know your novelist's protagonist as intimately as if you, the screenwriter, had invented the character yourself.

The faithful dramatist is wise, therefore, to answer searching questions about the protagonist's inner being. The answers contribute intimate details which provide the final touch for the audience . . . a depth of feeling. Our questions below apply to Claire, the protagonist of *Claire Serrat*.

QUESTIONING YOUR PROTAGONIST

Q. Who is she? Describe her appearance and personality.
Q. How does she speak and think?
Q. Where does she live?
Q. Where does she work? What does she do for a living?
Q. Who are her parents?
Q. Who are her friends, neighbors, lovers, coworkers?
Q. Does she have any unique characteristics? Mannerisms?
Q. How does she dress?

It is vital for a screenwriter to understand thoroughly the protagonist. Only through that understanding can the writer convey to the audience the intensity of emotion that will build the suspense of the screenplay and propel the story to its ultimate resolution. Yet the writer must bring insight and understanding to another character, one as important in the grand reach of the play as the protagonist—the antagonist. To increase your awareness of the thoughts, actions, gestures, and nuances of your antagonist, ask the same questions about the antagonist that you have just answered about the protagonist. The discussion that follows pertains to Martin, the antagonist of *Claire Serrat*.

QUESTIONING YOUR ANTAGONIST

Q. Who is he? Describe his appearance.
A. He is Martin. A man in his middle to late twenties, handsome and
    attractive, he lives in the strange belief that his dead mother, whom

he has buried, still communicates with him and guides and protects him. Moreover, she has told him that God has sent Claire to him for his needs, and that he must keep her and make her well. His resolve cannot be shaken.

Continue with the same questions you asked about the protagonist. As you reread the developing narrative of your novel leading up to the problem (backstory), make an insightful list of the character's values. Note any observable characteristics, such as traits and mannerisms, that give depth and substance to your antagonist.

Six

THE NATURE OF
A TREATMENT

In the interest of cogency, without which your play will suffer, you should at this point delineate for yourself exactly what this story means to you: that is, how do you want to treat it? What do you want to achieve in the telling of it? Why did you choose it?

The question is: Are you telling the story because the plot is highly diverting, or because it is entertaining in a mysterious sense, or because the leading characters are exceptionally colorful, bright, and charming? Or perhaps you're trying to illuminate a social or political idea or issue. Specifically what, in essence, are you trying to say?

Somewhere in your mind, the novel of your choice must have evolved around some specific concept. To that end, the plot of your play will grow out of that central thought; the scenes will grow out of the plot. The play will eventually emphasize this central purpose.

Now is the time to get a clear idea of the subject of your novel—what is it saying?—before you begin to write your treatment—the scene-by-scene development of your screenplay. If you managed earlier to articulate the theme of your novel, then that is what we're talking about now. Furthermore, when you have that theme in mind, anything which is not essential to the message—including characters, scenes, even subplots—should be eliminated.

Also, you should decide in your own mind at the outset whether your novel is a comedy or a drama—a farce or a tragedy. Don't attempt to combine them in any way, shape, or form. They just don't mix. This, of course, does not mean that you cannot include elements of humor or high comedy in a dramatic story. Indeed, a leitmotif serves to increase the effectiveness of the drama.

Now that we have distinguished between the plot of a novel and the plot of a play, we can proceed to the business of analyzing our story for the purpose of isolating the struggle that will challenge the protagonist for the duration of the play. This means you must now find that point in the story that quickly leads up to the protagonist's motivation to deal with the problem of the play.

THE POINT OF DEPARTURE

You are now determining the dramatic *center* of your play (the need of the protagonist to defend his or her values), as well as the dramatic *focus* of the play, namely, the protagonist's objective (the climax of the play, the scene in which he or she wins or loses). Hereafter, each step of your play, from the first scene to the last, must concern itself with that center (need) and that focus (objective).

With that in mind, let us ask questions that will help you find your play's point of departure.

Q. What is the difference between the novel and the play?

A. The novel pretends to be real. The play presumes to be happening; a happening is real.

Q. Why do the members of an audience accept this presumption? Do they actually believe that the play is real?

A. No; they certainly do not if they think about it.

Q. Then, what must be done to cause the viewers to suspend their disbelief that what they are looking at is real?

A. The playwright must make them *feel* what is happening.

Q. How do we make them feel?

A. We appeal to their emotions.

Q. How do you generate *feeling*, which is the catalyst that infuses the play with reality?

A. You generate that feeling by encouraging, or exciting the sympathy, empathy, or hostility of the audience. Hence, the play begins with the reaction of a character to a crisis. (Note: A dramatic play consists of a series of crises starting with the initial crisis, namely, the play's point of departure. The word *crisis* is also used to describe the end of Act II, that is, the main crisis.

Q. When we say that we must make the audience viewers *feel*, does that mean we don't want them to think?

A. Of course not. There are two levels at which the audience is involved in the play—the conscious and unconscious levels. At the conscious level, the people are thinking about the protagonist's problem, or dilemma. Unconsciously, they are sympathizing or empathizing with the protagonist's struggle. (Note: In order to create a situation in which a play is felt by the audience, it must be felt equally by the protagonist. The protagonist must not feel sympathy or empathy, however, as that is the audience's reaction, but anxiety as he or she reacts to the crisis. If the protagonist doesn't care about what's happening, why should the audience? Hence, the underlying vitality of the play exists in the feeling it generates for the audience.)

QUESTIONING YOUR POINT OF DEPARTURE: CLAIRE SERRAT

Q. What is the crisis in your novel that creates the play's point of departure? What motivates the protagonist?
A. Claire's crisis is the rupture of her love affair with Robert and her belief that she is dying from tuberculosis.
Q. Who is the antagonist?
A. Martin, a half-mad Provençale peasant, is the antagonist.
Q. What is the antagonist's objective?
A. Martin wants to possess Claire and keep her a captive in his deserted village.

Think about your answers before we proceed to write our treatment.

UNITY

We know that three issues of conflict may be experienced in drama. We may find two or even three of them in the same play. Ultimately, however, the issue of conflict that motivates the protagonist and which is eventually resolved in the climactic scene at the end of the play is the crucial issue of conflict.

Once you know the beginning and the end of your play, every subsequent step of its development—every scene or sequence of scenes—must be subordinated to that single action. We call this "straight-lining" the play—unifying through cause and effect.

Hence, each incident that you develop in the play, unlike the novel, must have the effect of moving the protagonist toward or away from the objective or goal. In other words, each incident moves to the climax. A causal connection must exist between each step, from the motivation to the resolution of the plot.

Failing to achieve that end, your play lacks the required element of *unity*. In dramatic terms, unity of action means that a play must have a single main plot and must be told from a single point of view. It follows that the unity of problem and conflict is tied to the protagonist.

A Significant Matter of Tense

A glaring error, frequently made by neophytes in the preparation of their treatments, is the use of the past tense. Never lose sight of the fact that the play takes place in the present. We are dealing with reality, and reality has nothing to do with the past. Remember, you are not telling the story the way the author did in the book; you are translating material into scenes of action (what the people are saying and doing), which reveals to the audience what the author was telling you in the book. Such lapses usually occur when you are writing the treatment.

Never say, "He *ate* his breakfast." He *eats* his breakfast. Never say, "He *went* to the office." He *goes to* the office. Never say, "He *told* her to stop." He *tells* her to stop.

With this in mind, you should approach Act I of your treatment with the parameters clearly in view. Namely, the beginning—where your people presently are—and the end—where your people presently will be. The opening scenes introduce the problem for the protagonist, and the closing scene of Act I establishes the issue of conflict.

Between these two points, judiciously follow the straight line of developing complications (that is, choices, decisions, and changes that appear to deteriorate with each new step).

Students inevitably ask: how long should this treatment be? Unless the writer plans to offer the treatment as an item for sale—in which case the style and quality of the material becomes a significant item—the treatment is an undertaking that is strongly suggested for the adapter's own guidance. The length of it depends entirely on personal preference as you consider your needs. My own experience has shown that writers who hastily go straight to the script invariably end with rewrites and revisions of the final screenplay that far outweigh the time that would have been better spent on a well-crafted, neatly prepared treatment.

TREATMENT FORMAT

In the treatment, you will follow the conventions of scriptwriting to assist you in your ultimate objective: writing a screenplay that meets the highest professional standards. In your treatment, introduce a character for the first time by placing the name in capital letters. Similarly, draw attention to such important elements as camera shots and sounds by placing the appropriate words in capital letters. You may want to refer to Chapter 9 for other scriptwriting conventions and information on camera language as well as to the Glossary for definitions of film terms that may be unfamiliar to you.

Seven

THE TREATMENT

Claire Serrat

by

I.A.R. Wylie

We OPEN on a PANORAMIC VIEW of the village of Draguignan in Provence, France. It is 1948. We pick up CLAIRE SERRAT'S English two-seater runabout as it threads its way through the town. It stops at a small, shabby hotel. Claire enters the hotel. CAMERA picks up a small truck that is leaving the village and follows it to ESTABLISH the surrounding valley, the hilly farmland, and the highway that moves in a straight line through the valley to the next town.

Along the highway, CAMERA HOLDS on a distant, ancient, washed-out bridge that was once the entrance to a now-deserted village. A rickety, broken road leads from the highway to the bridge. A sign on the highway reads: ROUTE BARRE.

We MOVE IN to examine the village and meet MARTIN. He, like the village, has a harsh look of survival from disaster. The aura of unreality that cloaks this secretive place is also cast upon him. He peers through narrowed eyes with the intentness of a wild animal to whom every sound and movement has significance. Bared to the waist, his weathered and embattled face is that of a boy plunged too suddenly into manhood.

Martin proceeds to a cemetery where his mother is buried. Her grave is singularly well-kept among all the other relics. He converses with her as if she were alive. This done, he proceeds through the abandoned streets to the village square, where he perches on the wall to look out over the valley and the distant highway.

Slowly, his eyes darken as he sees a small speck of an auto crazily careening along the abandoned, broken cart road toward the washed-out bridge and its destruction. The car is Claire's two-seater runabout.

We CUT TO the car as Claire cries "Robert . . . oh, Robert," and crashes through the void and into the gully below.

Martin, confused and uncertain, slowly makes his way laboriously to the tattered thing of flesh and blood that is Claire. And as he uncovers her face, we DISSOLVE TO:

DR. FENWICK's office. We are in the English village that bears Claire's name—Serrat County. Here old Dr. John, the retired family doctor, confirms what Claire's Harley Street doctors have already told her—she has advanced tuberculosis. Besides, she is trying to kill herself. Why?

Claire bitterly reflects how her father died in a fire he set to burn their mansion because he could no longer keep it after the war, and how her brother had given his life to that war. Later her mother took her own life, as well.

But Dr. John says that there's still hope if Claire behaves and gets lots of rest and good food.

"I know a small hotel in Draguignan," Claire says.

"That's in Provence, the south of France," Dr. John declares. "An excellent place."

"Once it was blissful," says Claire.

Now, we CUT to a scrubby, one-room flat in a back-street London house. Alone and lonely, Claire is visited by her father, LORD SERRAT. He has come to give her some valuable estate pieces which he has taken from the manor, now closed. The money will help her, he says, but from now on, she must learn to depend on herself. "Strike new roots," he says as he leaves.

As she wonders miserably where to begin, there is an imperative knock on her door. It is ROBERT entering her life. And, although he is living with CANDY, his present target is Claire.

Now, we go back to Draguignan and our opening scene as Claire threads her way through the town and stops in front of the small hotel. This time, she gets out of the car and enters.

Seated in the restaurant of the hotel, Claire overhears a group of ARTISTS and a NORTHERN INTELLECTUAL discussing the restoration of an old deserted village with its half-ruined castle and fine frescoes in the chapel. The group has heard that only one inhabitant is left, a half-mad peasant.

But we learn from the PATRONNE that Claire is not a welcome guest. She was here before—with her lover. But at least she did not cough all night. "I do not like my guests to be disturbed," the patronne says resentfully.

Having overheard this—which, indeed, was the Patronne's malicious intention—is enough for Claire to question the meaninglessness of her existence. She leaves, and now we SEE her little car driving along the highway on the valley floor. She approaches the broken, rickety road and the sign: ROUTE BARRE. And as she turns onto the road leading to the washed-out bridge. BACK TO:

Claire, who finally regains consciousness. We are in Martin's room, where we learn that some time has passed since the accident. Claire has survived through Martin's ministrations. Martin tells Claire that his mother told him how to care for her and save her life.

Claire's long, thick, black hair has been rudely hacked short. She is covered with cuts, bruises, and scars as she lies naked under a coarse, gray sheet in a tattered bed. Her delirious eyes rove about the weirdly patched room with its single broken window.

Martin, half-naked and with his brilliant visionary stare, looks monstrous. Gradually it becomes evident that Claire is paralyzed from the waist down.

Slowly, carefully, Claire tries to find out who Martin is and where she is. All of her fears are magnified when she learns that Martin has been treating her, and there is no doctor. She is momentarily encouraged when Martin refers to his mother's advice—only to learn that she is dead.

Hysterically, Claire tries to make sense out of her own madness, but Martin can only respond with his brand of reason.

We cover the passage of time photographically: the countryside, the distant highway, the insularity, the remoteness, the washed-out bridge, the square, the lavoir. And, through it all, a tormented Claire tries every conceivable means of convincing Martin that he cannot and must not keep her a prisoner—that he must return her to her people. But her lamentations only seem to trouble him; he cannot be distracted from his mother's wish.

Eventually, a more relaxed Martin is attending a healthier albeit unapologetically unpleasant, indignant, resentful Claire. When she pleads for Martin to kill her, he responds by scolding her for her godlessness.

Meanwhile, as she grows stronger, she becomes more courageous, believing that in time she will find his weakness. Then, one day, Martin appears vulnerable: he believes he is entitled to some respect for his efforts. Claire shrieks, "I will never be grateful to you! Don't you understand? Never! Why do you keep me here?

And Martin responds, "You are all I have."

FADE OUT.

END ACT I

ACT II

The summer heat comes, and Martin carries Claire out to the village square. Wrapped in a sheet, she struggles and rails at him as he places her on a mattress beneath a broad plane tree. Only the crumbling buildings silence her. Now, for the first time, she examines the surrounding village. She asks Martin why no one comes here. And when she accuses him of hiding from the law, he leaves abruptly in anger. But that night, fearful in the strange stillness of this eerie place, she calls to him. And he comes, bringing her a warm dinner that he has specially cooked for her that evening.

Though she continues to protest his every kindness, her health continues to improve. We can see that the scars are gone, and Martin remarks, "You are not coughing anymore." But when Martin observes, "Your hair—it is beautiful," Claire coldly replies, "What do you know of beauty?"

"I lived once with a city woman," he replies. "She was beautiful—like you."

That night, we find Martin in a decayed, disintegrated barn. By lantern light, with a knife in his hand, he is tending to the needs of a mother goat. Suddenly he freezes; something has alerted him. He rises and quickly EXITS the barn. We CUT to Claire in bed; she is writhing in the toils of some agony as Martin appears in the doorway. The piercing pain is from an earache.

Maman has told Martin how to help. Laying his knife on the floor, he makes a poultice. In her agony, Claire is grateful and, for the first time, gracious. When sleep comes, Martin sits at the edge of the bed worshiping her slumber.

When morning comes, the fever is gone. Claire sees Martin asleep on the edge of the bed—and, on the floor, his knife. Stealthily she reaches for it and gets it. She manages to conceal it just as Martin wakes.

Martin explains that he will take this day to go to the valley for needed things, but she is not to worry: "Maman will watch over you."

This ignites Claire's fury. "Your mother is dead!" she shouts. "And you're mad!" She swiftly raises the knife to plunge it into her breast, but Martin snatches it and slaps a stinging blow across her face. "It does not matter what you say to me," he says, "but to take your life is an offense against God." This said, he lifts her with her sheet and carries her outside.

As Claire lies in her usual place, Martin gives her an old Bible. This leads them into their first civil conversation. Martin wants to know about Claire's life. And she tells him. He asks about the man Robert, whose name she has often uttered and for whom he has a curious contempt.

Also he wheels out a contraption he has made—an armchair with two large wooden wheels attached. And now, for the first time, Claire is exhilarated as she tries it.

Martin takes her to see the village: the main street with its stores, the church with its bell in the tower (the bell that Maman rings when she wants to talk to Martin), the schoolhouse and its schoolroom where he sat as a child—and the cemetery and Maman. Here, Martin introduces Claire. "See how well she looks," he tells Maman. As they leave, Claire places her hand on the grave and says, "Goodbye, Madame."

That night, as Claire pretends to be asleep in her bed on the square, she glances surreptitiously across the ground to where Martin lies in his customary place on the grass. She knows he is looking at her, and she senses his mood as he gets up and begins to pace restlessly. Finally, he approaches her and raises his hand as if to lay it upon her. SIMULT, a violent gust of wind blows across the square causing the bell in the tower to toll. Martin snatches his hand back. He pauses for a moment then walks into the shadows. And the storm increases in its violence. All of nature seems to grow furious. Claire opens her eyes, imploring, "Oh, God, let me escape!"

But the wind grows fiercer, flailing the animals in its fury: the BELL TOLLS LOUDER until, finally, with a horrifying crash, the bell falls to the ground.

Panic-stricken, Claire struggles to pull herself up, and, miraculously, her body responds. Incredulous, she falls back on the bed as Martin appears, shouting, "The bell! The devil has torn down her bell! Now, she will never call me again!"

Making no sign of her condition, she tries to calm him and persuades him to carry her back to the room.

The next day, Claire waits in trepidation until Martin leaves. Then she tries her legs and is ecstatic when they respond. Next, she goes to the armoire where Martin has placed her clothes and possessions. She checks her purse, her passport, her money—everything is in order, as it was. Then, as she sees Martin returning with his pail of water and rags for her daily bath, she jumps back into bed.

When he reaches for the sheet to strip her, Claire forgetfully now clings to it, shouting, "For the love of God leave me alone." But, in response, she sees Martin's suspicious eye; he appears to sense that something has changed— something is different.

In an effort to beguile him, Claire, now pleasant, changes the subject: "You say I'm beautiful. Bring me a mirror so I can see what I look like."

He does. And now, for the first time since the crash, she closes her eyes to conjure the vision of what she looked like. And, in the mirror, we FLASHBACK to the vision of Claire as we saw her in Dr. John's mirror. Only we are seeing her reflection not in Dr. John's office mirror but in the makeup mirror in Robert's elegant backstage dressing room. Claire is alone and looking at herself in the mirror when there is a knock on the door. Claire opens it and is surprised to find Candy smiling at her. After two years, she has come to see Claire. But Candy's gay smile abruptly turns sour as she reacts to the sight of Claire. Knowing Robert's self-centered character, she agonizes over what he has done to Claire. And when Claire says that Robert will be back in a moment from a telephone call with his New York agent, Candy says that she would rather not wait.

Candy leaves, and Robert returns in the next instant with good news: a Hollywood movie. "We have worlds to conquer, my darling," he tells Claire.

But Claire has had enough. "I don't want to drag around on your coattails. Leave me behind."

"You know I won't leave you behind. And let's have no further word about it," Robert declares. He storms out, slamming the door.

We return to the present with Claire still looking in the mirror. She turns to Martin. His eyes no longer have their secret look of preoccupation. Instead, as though aware of some change which he cannot yet capture, he has become watchful. He stares as if admiring Claire for the first time. "Maman was pretty, too," he says.

Claire tries to change the subject. "But there are other women, M'sieur Martin. There was that city woman you loved."

Then, suddenly, like the terrible explosion of a too-long-contained agony, Martin cries: "I killed her!"

There is a deathly silence.

FADE OUT.

END ACT II

ACT III

Claire, continuing her masquerade, lies on her pallet on the square, covertly watching Martin as he sits on the rampart wall. His eyes no longer have their secret look of preoccupation; he has become watchful.

Soon he exits, explaining that there are things he must do outside; he will be gone all day.

When he leaves, Claire breathes her first sigh of relief. Warily, she raises herself and slips off the bed. Peering over the wall in Martin's direction, she sees that he is a large speck in the distance.

Now, she tests her legs. She walks in measured steps toward the desolate street. Curiously, she examines this place that has been her home for so long; something compels her to visit the cemetery to say goodbye to Martin's mother. But her confidence snaps, and she hurries back to the square. The experience leaves her more exhausted than she had expected. She lies on the bed, panting and shaken. Her strength completely gone, she falls asleep.

And now it is NIGHT. We SEE a man on the deserted street, framed in a shot from the legs down: modern brown shoes, trousers smartly belted at the waist. The hair is neatly trimmed; the face is cleanly shaved. When his back is in full view of the camera, we SEE he is well-built and grace-ful as he moves toward the plane tree in the square.

As he raises his lamp over Claire's head, she stirs and opens her eyes. They fill with terror at the sight of him. "Here I am," he says shyly. It is Martin.

Claire's terror becomes a mystified silence as he explains that he has brought several things back from Draguignan. He brings forth a housecoat. Maman said it will give her pleasure. But though he still talks of Maman, his eyes no longer search her dully but look directly and appealingly at her.

He explains that today he bought things for their personal use, but tomorrow he will get other things they need. He brings forth other things to celebrate this night.

The following morning we OPEN on Martin's room as Claire bursts in frantically. It is clear that Martin has already left, and this is her opportunity.

She pulls open the armoire and removes her clothes and her possessions. She dresses quickly and exits the room. Looking in every crevice, she makes her way to the square, where she crouches at the wall and peers over the edge. So far as the eyes can see, no one is there. Tears fill her eyes as she starts for the street. She reaches the path leading down to the ravine and starts her stumbling descent to her final freedom. Halfway down, she makes a sharp turn in the road and meets Martin coming up on the other side.

Claire stands momentarily petrified and speechless as Martin measures her with a new and terrible intensity. Then, in a sudden fury, he seizes her as she claws violently at him.

Despite all her protestations, he carries her back to his room, where he flings his package down on the bed. In a mad frenzy, he tears off her clothes and lays the burden of his panting body on Claire. And she resists with all her strength. But eventually she responds with desire for Martin, her resistance becomes an embrace, and we FADE OUT.

FADE IN to discover Martin seated on the rampart wall. As he overlooks the valley, we can detect a sharply different presence of mind—and an austere peace.

Claire, now wearing Maman's black dress, approaches him. In a kind, forgiving conversation they review their time together and the vast differences that separate their lives and their worlds.

Martin knows that there is no place for him in Claire's life, and he prepares to help her in the arduous task of reaching the highway and her freedom.

Along the way, Claire probes to learn Martin's story and how he killed the woman he loved. It is a heartbreaking story, and not a murder. But it left him with a broken mind.

Finally, they reach the highway where Claire will wait for a lift to Draguignan. As Martin makes his way back to the village, a small car containing two of the artists we met in the beginning pulls up beside him. They explain the purpose of their mission and begin to question Martin. As Martin hesitates to reveal himself, Claire returns to protect him.

However, when they learn who Martin is, they recall his family—a well-known family—and now it appears he will be useful. And so will Claire, if, as they question, she belongs in Draguignan, too.

As Martin stands by silently, Claire ponders the question. Finally, Claire responds: "Yes. I belong here, too." And they all go off together to examine what must be done to renew the village.

THE END

Eight

DIALOGUE

A dramatist is a juggler with three balls in the air: plot, character, and dialogue. Elaborating on that image, one might say that when the dramatist deals with dialogue alone, he is more like a magician. The trick, you might say, is: Now you see it; now you don't.

The principal aim of good dialogue is to convey clearly and succinctly the information that the audience must know in order to be continually involved in the story. But, far more important, these utterances must reveal the characters' feelings, both apparent and hidden. In other words, while the ostensible purpose of dialogue is to advance the plot, the dialogue should not simply state the facts of the story.

When the characters in a play are used by the writer for the sole purpose of developing the plot in dialogue form rather than living through the experience, the audience senses immediately that the characters are artificial—they are not talking like real people. And this is the inevitable result when the writer is so bound to the facts of the novel that he or she imagines rather than feels the scene that is being written.

Dialogue is genuine only when it grows out of the emotions of the character. The audience is more interested in the character than it is in the situation itself. In short, the dialogue should present not the situation itself, but rather the situation as it is felt by the characters who are experiencing it.

Thus, the analysis of your characters is critically important. If you truly know the emotional composition of each individual, you will find for them the words that describe how they feel. This is what you derive from the amalgam of values and traits that you have extracted from the novel.

In actuality, while dialogue might seem to be the least difficult part of your job, it requires the most precise and painstaking attention. Professionals occasionally refer to it as the "jewelry work"—dialogue is to be examined as closely as a jeweler examines a rare gem under a loupe.

This point cannot be stressed too seriously. Although you may have brought brilliant originality to the highly emotional problems being resolved in a meaningful story, your dialogue must convey these qualities through simple, everyday conversation that reflects the emotional context of the speaker, or the creative work will be totally vitiated.

Since it is a matter of the greatest importance that you translate your play's vital information into the language of casual conversation, let us examine conversational characteristics.

All of our daily conversation is informal by nature and made of large doses of slang expressions, colloquialisms, and, more often than not, inelegant expressions. Indeed, we regard a person as being unique when he or she uses carefully chosen words and phrases that are grammatically and syntactically correct. Many people also associate ornateness in speech with the foreign-born.

Normally we don't think out a sentence in advance when we speak the way we do when we write. There's nothing unusual about a written sentence that says: "As he ran down the corridor, Dr. Baker, who is not very athletic, tripped over his own foot and took a header."

The student who described the incident said it this way: "Y'know what happened to Dr. Baker? He took a header. Running down the corridor— tripped on his own foot. He's not very athletic."

Also, unless we use two words for the sake of emphasis, such as "I will," or three words, such as "I will not," we use contractions wherever possible. We say: "I'll" for "I will," "can't" for "cannot," and so on. Often we leave sentences unfinished. Either we lose track of what we wanted to say, or we are interrupted by someone with another idea, and we never get to the point.

For example: "Guess what happened to Doc Baker?"

"Who?"

"Baker. You know—math."

"Oh, yeah. That reminds me, did you work out that third problem?"

This is the effect you must achieve. This is the magic: an illusion of everyday speech which is unsurpassed in direction, purpose, and syntax. In other words, good dialogue must (A) sound conversational, (B) suit the characters, (C) reveal their values and traits, and (D) advance the plot. And it must accomplish all of these with the most economical, minimal choices of words.

On the whole, you will be on safe ground if you shorten any sentence that is long and keep all speeches as lean and as brief as possible. If a character's speech can be delivered by a character other than the one from whom it was written, that dialogue is defective.

The essence of drama is drawn from the fact that audiences care more for the human being trapped in a situation than they do for the situation itself. Only when the situation is presented not for the situation itself but for the way in which it is felt by the characters will it hold their interest.

Good dialogue is the simplest expression of a character's emotions. These emotions should be obvious and ordinary. Given a free rein, the characters' emotions will find the appropriate words to express themselves.

ECONOMY OF DIALOGUE

When we discussed plotting the novel, your attention was called to the fact that you must diligently avoid any scene that does not move the story forward or throw some additional light on the characters and their situation. If what you are depicting adds no new development, the scene will in all likelihood end up on the cutting-room floor when the picture is edited.

Here again, in dialogue, reconsider that precaution. Always exclude excessive words, phrases, and speeches that go beyond dramatic need (that is, giving the play meaning). Except where the verbosity of a character is a trait or where speech is used for ornament, limit each character to the leanest, most economical use of words.

AUTHENTICITY AND DIALECTS

Unless you use the terms and phrases of characters who commonly have a special style of language that an audience familiarly associates with such people, your characters will fail to have the ring of authenticity. Although such authenticity is customarily taken care of by the novelist, it is occasionally neglected.

Then there is the other side of the coin. The writer whose characters use the highly technical language of their trades and professions—scientists, doctors, and lawyers, for example—shouldn't worry about whether the audience understands the terms. It is only important that the audience hears the ring of authenticity.

Another precaution regarding dialects concerns excessive direction. Authors often attempt to indicate the pronunciation of dialects by spelling them out for the reader. In drama, such a procedure is more hurtful than helpful, because it makes the script arduous to read and difficult to understand. The actor or actress who is chosen for the part will probably have an aptitude for dialect. If not, no amount of phoneticizing will help him or her to sound like the genuine article.

On the other hand, some authors have the knack of structuring speeches in the fashion of the idiom. If they do, use their work as your starting point. If they don't, you as adapter should assume the responsibility for doing so. For example, an Irishman in a play might say, "'Tis a fine time we'll be havin' at the party." That sentence is better and easier to read than, "We'll shore hev a foin toim at the pahrrty."

Another grievance among actors is a writer who constantly describes the manner in which each speech is supposed to be spoken. It is not uncommon to find an endless array of descriptions, such as "angrily," "idly," "sadly," "flatly," and "happily," with the most startling suggestion being "naturally." This habit is mostly an indulgence of beginners. Be wise: don't tip your mitt.

Only when the meaning of a speech is not clear in the normal reading of a line is it useful to include an instruction. Here's an example:

WIFE
Won't it be nice to see my mother again?

HUSBAND
(drearily)
Yes, dear, I can hardly wait.

In short, a speech should speak for itself. If a line that calls for anger or sadness is not provoked by the situation, look to the motivation rather than the speech description.

TAG LINES AND CURTAIN LINES

Writing tag lines and curtain lines may be the most demanding skill that is expected of you. A *tag line* is the closing speech in a scene. A *curtain line* is the closing speech of an act. In each case, such a speech should tersely gather all the emotional power of the scene or the act into a final focus.

Obviously, a curtain line needs more attention than a tag line. In point of fact, there may be times when a scene doesn't warrant a tag line, but a curtain line must always have power.

This again brings up the importance of dividing the play into three acts—beginning, middle, and end. We mentioned that there is no evidence of act endings in screenplays. Television scripts and stageplays may indicate two acts or ten acts, depending upon their length. Don't let this unnerve you. No matter how many acts are designated, there are still only three structural acts to every play.

Summing up, the stage is a playground, not a pulpit; characters talk, they don't make speeches; a scene is a setting where commonplace words are used dexterously. Good dialogue states the facts with the most refreshing use of language and demands a sensitive grasp of the emotional significance of each sequence of action, which is consistent with the characters' values and traits.

Nine

CAMERA LANGUAGE AND SCREENPLAY FORMAT

Some members of the film industry disagree about the extent of the film writer's responsibilities—indeed, prerogatives—as they relate to the matter of photographing the story. Even my university colleagues find it difficult to draw a line between how little or how much photographic detail is considered a reasonable exercise of the writer's province.

First, we must dispose of a warped philosophy in cinema arts, too often expressed in film-study courses, that film is a director's medium. Nothing could be more misleading.

Admittedly, in theatrical films, more so than in television, the director's creative contribution to the artistic sense of a film is paramount. But the writer's contribution to the process is equally vital. Most films would never see the light of day were it not for the writer—that individual who creates and provides the first full screenplay which makes all the additional contributions feasible. Thus, the first final script is and should be the writer's photographic version of the play.

But the more I defend the writer's point of view, the more I sense an infatuation among students with irrelevant angles and shots that have a tendency to muddy the story and dilute the script's readability. The present trend of thought favors the most economical use of camera instructions in the script. In television, where time is money and production costs are astronomical, this position is a difficult one to challenge. Sophisticated camera instructions are not highly regarded in a marketplace where the chief concern is the clock.

Unless there is a relationship between the writer and the buyer, the single most important factor that influences the reading of an unknown script is the look and feel of professionalism. This is most clearly revealed in the format of the script and the use of the camera.

Any intelligent discussion of camera coverage must therefore stress the advantages and the disadvantages of each of these views. On balance, it appears reasonable to say that the camera should not be called into play except when it is used to provide meaningful dramatic value. The fact is, we are talking about making movies, and the language of the camera is the heart of the play. The language is not difficult. The basic purpose of a script is not just to present dialogue; it is a guide to the separate activities of a large number of people who are engaged in the process of producing it. Properly written, the script focuses the attention of these diverse departments on their own individual but collaborative contributions.

To this end, your script serves two purposes: first, it tells a story; second, it is a blueprint, or a set of instructions, for those people involved in the filming of it. The best instructions are brief, clear, cogent, and do not clutter or confuse the story.

The screenplay *Claire Serrat* appears in the format most widely used at both the film studios and the networks. Nonetheless, there is no single way to present a script. So long as the script lucidly, simply, and accurately describes the transition of the story from concept to film, it fulfills its job. Variations exist; the script might even take the form of a letter.

However, the preference for uniformity is twofold. First, a good script uses common language which doesn't require a translation. More importantly, though, a script that conforms to industry standards provides the best opportunity for the practiced eye of the reader to envision the movie. It is, to that extent, a storyboard.

Today, the *shot-for-shot technique* is the most common approach used in writing screenplays. In it, the writer outlines the shots to be used as the screenplay progresses as a way of telling the story. The principal service that the shot-for-shot technique provides is the opportunity for the writer to deliver the most effective visual treatment of the dramatic elements of the play.

The substance of a film may also be set forth in another method using what are called *master scenes*. In this procedure, the writer simply establishes the scene and thereafter chiefly focuses on the characters and the dialogue without considering the placement of the camera or the moves that may be necessary to detail the action. The serious dramatist, however, is usually not satisfied with such a format and generally does not consider this kind of script a finished product. Whether the shot-for-shot technique or the master-scene method is used, though, the careful writer uses the camera for the single purpose of conveying the *dramatic values* of the story, not to demonstrate artistic directorial suggestions.

In short, a writer who does not visualize each foot of film in relationship to the camera is like a painter without a canvas. The dramatist's canvas is the camera frame. As a film writer, you are telling a story by means of images. The old adage, "Don't say it; show it," is more than a caution: it is the meaning of film.

This is the dramatist's obligation—to use the camera in such a way that the viewer properly evaluates what the dramatist sees. The audience might not see the dramatist's concept of reality at all unless the writer focuses its attention on it.

In order, therefore, to manipulate the camera and properly instruct it in obtaining these dramatic values, we need to become acquainted not only with its placement and how it may be moved but also with the nomenclature that is used to achieve these objectives. Whenever you describe in your script the angle of placement or the movement of the camera, you are addressing not only the director but also the camera operator and assistants, the gaffer (lighting electrician), and the key grips. For that reason, always capitalize their instructions in the script. This also means you capitalize the word SEE when you want the camera to SEE something.

CAMERA LANGUAGE

It is unlikely that you will want to use all of the wide variety of camera shots that are available to you, but for the sake of familiarity, let us learn to recognize some of the most common with their abbreviations. Additional camera terms may be found in the Glossary. But remember—the present tendency in writing for the screen is to limit camera instructions as much as possible and leave judgment to the director.

Some of the most common shots relate to the distance between the camera and its subject:

CLOSE is a general direction for a camera shot to be taken from a close distance from the subject. This term allows quite a bit of latitude and is less specific than either CLOSE SHOT or CLOSE-UP.

CLOSE SHOT (CS) is a close angle of two or more elements close to the viewer.

CLOSE-UP (CU) is a tight shot that focuses clearly on an individual, usually from the waist up. It is not to be confused with a close shot.

EXTREME CLOSE-UP (ECU) is invariably a head shot or a tighter CU.

FULL SHOT (FS) is used to established the entire scene for the purpose of orientation.

LONG SHOT (LS) is taken at a considerable distance from the viewer to the subject, but, unlike the full shot, shows only that portion of the scene which you specifically want the viewer to see.

MEDIUM SHOT (MS) or MED. SHOT is taken from a distance that is neither long nor close. It is a middle distance from the camera to the subject.

Some shots refer to the number of characters in the image. Examples are TWO SHOTS, THREE SHOTS, and GROUP SHOTS.

Some camera terms refer to movement:

MOVING SHOTS follow the action that they are photographing. For example: MOVING SHOT CADILLAC describes the camera following an automobile in motion.

Other camera terms show movements that modify a shot while it is on the screen.

DOLLY IN and DOLLY OUT direct the camera operator to move the camera closer to or further from the subject.

PAN instructs the camera to move from left to right.

TILT tells the camera to move up or down.

ZOOM IN and ZOOM OUT increase or decrease the field of vision of the camera without moving the camera, relying on the ZOOMAR lens. Much use is made today of this specialized lens.

The experienced screenwriter also is familiar with shots that show angles:

FAVORING ANGLES select the character to be favored in the shot.

HIGH ANGLES instruct the camera to shoot down from above the subject.

LOW ANGLES tell the camera to shoot up from below the subject.

OVERHEAD SHOTS look down at the subject, such as a pool table.

OVER THE SHOULDER angles involve shooting from behind a character, over the shoulder, to see the expression of one person as two characters face each other.

POINT OF VIEW (POV) gives the audience a close look at what the person in the scene is looking at. This is usually preceded by a CLOSE SHOT of the individual who is looking in the direction of his or her own POV.

REVERSE ANGLE is a shot opposite of the preceding angle.

Some scenes involve laboratory procedures:

CUTS are scene or shot changes on the screen. These are done automatically in the laboratory, and the writer does not need to indicate them. Nonetheless, writers occasionally indicate CUT TO or SMASH CUT to communicate a certain feeling to the reader of the script.

DISSOLVE is another lab procedure, now considered outdated. It is an optical effect of bringing a picture in while collaterally fading the previous picture out.

FADE IN and FADE OUT are transitions that have the effect of raising and lowering "curtains" on a screenplay. FADE IN brightens a bland screen to a full picture, while FADE OUT is a dimming to complete darkness.

SHARED SCREEN or SPLIT SCREEN gives the effect of wiping half the picture off the screen and replacing that half with another picture.

SUPERIMPOSITION (SUPER) gives the effect of blending one picture or caption on top of another.

SCRIPT EXAMPLES

Three script examples follow, each written using the shot-for-shot technique. The first example gives camera and format instructions written in professional script form. The other two examples show how characters are introduced, scenes are developed, and camera language is used properly in standard film format. Notice that each script reveals as quickly as it can the who, what, when, where, and how of the situation presented. Also notice that the time is given only when the scene is set; it is not used for any of the shots. Since shots take place only within scenes, the time has already been established when the scene opens. One last word: in the name of economy, avoid the excessive use of shots. A plethora of pointless shots, such as covering every character with a CU where a TWO-SHOT would serve the purpose, can be laborious and annoying and also can reveal your lack of experience to the professional reader.

Now, starting in each with the words FADE IN, let us see how the various components of a script work together.

First Example

FADE IN:

EXT.   STREET SCENE   DAY

Every scene of the play is set in the above fashion. In this space, you briefly describe the setting for the set designer and the prop person. You call their attention to things that must be supplied by putting the words in CAPITAL LETTERS. You introduce characters as they appear for the first time in the play by using CAPS. So, we meet the CHARACTER here, and give a brief description so the casting director will know your conception. Also, any SOUNDS for the sound effects technician (other than source sounds) are capitalized.

> CHARACTER
> (any tonal directions)
> All speeches are single-spaced, and if there
> is a pause in the dialogue, you do this . . .
> (beat)
> . . . and then continue the speech.

MED. SHOT   CHARACTER AND PAL

Now, we introduce PAL (note use of capital letters) as he ENTERS. He is a short, bearded prospector.

CONTINUED

CONTINUED

> PAL
> (timidly)
> His speech is typed in the same limits as
> the speech above.

ANOTHER ANGLE

This is the way you get a different look at the same shot. (For example, you may want to favor the character.)

> CHARACTER
> Now you go on with the dialogue and
> develop your situation.

CLOSE SHOT   PAL

CLOSE SHOTS are used for dramatic effect, to show important details, or to emphasize the importance of what is being said.

CU   CHARACTER

A CU, or CLOSE-UP, differs from a CLOSE SHOT in that it is always a head shot, whereas the CLOSE SHOT may be on a person or thing. For purposes of visual clarity, the common practice is to orient the audience first to the total scene and thereafter cover the details more closely and intimately with shots and angles.

Second Example

FADE IN:

EXT.   WASHINGTON D.C.   (STOCK SHOT)   NIGHT

HIGH AERIAL ESTABLISHING SHOT, emphasizing the nation's capitol with its light-enhanced dome.

EXT.   A STREET   (PENNSYLVANIA AVENUE)   NIGHT

LONG SHOT   CAPITOL DOME IN BG

MOVING SHOT   CLOSE ON TRUCK

as it comes to a halt. We can SEE TWO MEN sitting in the cab.

INT.   CAB OF TRUCK   NIGHT

The TRUCK DRIVER is a pleasant-looking, middle-aged, nondescript character whom we'll never see again. Next to him sits GIFFORD

CONTINUED

CONTINUED

JACKSON. Gifford, despite his country-bumpkin appearance, is a nice-looking, likeable, lanky young lad with a sunny disposition who could be anywhere between 20 and 25 years of age. A cute mongrel dog with soulful eyes sits at Gifford's feet with its paws on his knees.

> TRUCK DRIVER
> Well, Gifford, this is as close as I can take
> you to your destination. From here on,
> you and . . .
>> (smiling at dog and ruffling its
>> head)
> Miss Jones here are on your own.
>> (he points OS)
> There's the seat of our government.

Gifford looks os.

GIFFORD'S POV: CAPITOL IN THE DISTANCE

> TRUCK DRIVER'S
> VOICE (OS)
> (continuing)
> . . . and you'll find the Senate Building
> somewheres around there.

LONG SHOT   THE TRUCK

We SEE Gifford, carrying a small suitcase, get out of the truck. Miss Jones jumps out after him. Gifford exchanges some pleasantries and goodbyes with the truck driver. (MOS from this distance) and closes the cab door. As the truck roars off, Gifford waving to the driver, we

> DISSOLVE TO:

INT.   U.S. SENATE BUILDING   NIGHT

A CORRIDOR

CAMERA SHOOTS DOWN the fairly long, nightlit corridor with closed office doors on each side, then ZOOMS IN ON Gifford, sprawled out in front of one of the doors, his head resting on his suitcase. He's asleep. Miss Jones is stretched out at his feet, snoring gently. CAMERA MOVES IN ON SIGN ON DOOR which reads: SENATOR LUCIUS WALEBROOM.

BACK TO SCENE

CONTINUED

CONTINUED

as, from OS, comes the SOUND of approaching, RATHER UNEVEN FOOT-STEPS. Gifford stirs, slowly opens his eyes, looking sleepily down the dimly lit corridor as the FOOTSTEPS COME CLOSER.

GIFFORD'S POV
From way down the length of the corridor comes the senator.

Third Example

FADE IN:

EXT.   SLUM AREA   NIGHT

A section of dreary tenement buildings.

CLOSER ANGLE   ONE OF THE TENEMENT BUILDINGS

WYLIE's car is at the curb. He's examining the mailboxes in the door-way. Finding the one he wants, he enters the building.

INT.   TENEMENT BUILDING HALLWAY   NIGHT

as Wylie emerges from the stairway, looks around at the numbers on the doors, moves to one, and presses the bell.

CLOSER ANGLE   THE DOOR

There's no response to the bell. Wylie raps with his knuckles. After a moment, the door opens. A woman (MRS. LANDRY) is partially visible.

> WYLIE
> Mrs. Landry?

> MRS. LANDRY
> Who are you?

> WYLIE
> Edward Wylie. I don't know if you
> remember.

> MRS. LANDRY
> (harshly)
> I remember.

Notice that the time is given only when the scene is set; it is not used for any of the SHOTS. Since SHOTS only take place within a scene, the time has already been established when the scene opens.

One last word. In the name of economy, I urge you to avoid the excessive use of SHOTS. A plethora of pointless SHOTS such as covering every character with a CU where a TWO SHOT would serve the purpose can be laborius, annoying, and possibly revealing to the reader.

Part 2
THE SCREENPLAY

CLAIRE SERRAT

Screenplay by
Ben Brady
Based on the novel by
I. A. R. Wylie

FADE IN:

EXT. DRAGUIGNAN DAY (ESTABLISHING)

A panoramic view of the small Provençal town of
Draguignan, in the south of France. It is a bright, cool
spring morning. As CAMERA MOVES IN to the heart of the
town,

SUPERIMPOSE: DRAGUIGNAN

A town in Provence

1947

SUPER: MAIN TITLES

Now we are looking at the plane-tree-shaded SQUARE of the
town. We SEE and HEAR the colorful brouhaha of the market
place—the women's shrill voices raised in friendly argu-
ments, the clatter of wooden heels on cobbles, the clip-clop
of donkeys' hooves.

TITLES (SUPERIMPOSED)

A small canvas-topped two-seater English auto, of 1940s
vintage, the top down, becomes the center focus of the
scene. (It is CLAIRE SERRAT's car; we shall see it again later.)
CAMERA FOLLOWS as the car threads its way through the town
and stops in front of a small, nondescript hotel.

CONTINUED

CONTINUED

Although CAMERA is too distant for identification, Claire gets out of the car and enters the hotel. Meanwhile, under the striped hotel awning, a MAN is purchasing something from a VENDOR at one of the many marble-topped tables there.

He finishes, gets into a small truck, and drives off. CAMERA RISES, WIDENING THE ANGLE, FOLLOWING the truck through the town as it goes. It reaches the outskirts and proceeds upon a long, paved two-lane highway that stretches in a straight line north through the valley.

As CAMERA HOLDS on the small truck growing smaller in the distance, we ESTABLISH:

EXT.   THE VALLEY OF PROVENCE   DAY

A panoramic view of the hilly farmland which is divided by the two-lane highway that stretches like a ribbon along the valley floor. It is the route from Georges de Verden to Draguignan and on southward to the coast.

The countryside is fertile with large patches of early spring wheat. An abundance of grass and hyacinth are fanned by the wind.

As an occasional car speeds on its way, CAMERA discovers the approaching small truck. As the TRUCK passes closely BELOW CAMERA, a single sheet of paper appears to fly out of it. The paper floats upward in the breeze and then drifts lazily back to the highway.

CAMERA MOVES IN to read the paper, a single page from a calendar. The language is French. It indicates the month of April in the year 1947.

Suddenly, the wind picks up the sheet again and lifts it high above the ground. CAMERA RISES above it as it drifts upward, WIDENING THE ANGLE and following the sheet of paper as it is carried away from the highway toward a distant plateau.

IN CAMERA VIEW, the paper flies over the hills until it approaches a strange, secluded area which lies adjacent to but distant from the highway. It looks like the eerie ghost of a haunted, dead village. Now the paper loses its importance

CONTINUED

CONTINUED

and drifts out of view. CAMERA DESCENDS to examine the outskirts of the village and MOVES IN on an ancient, washed-out BRIDGE.

The decayed remains of the bridge have fallen into a precipitously steep gully that is now so wildly overgrown as to be well-nigh impenetrable. It evidently was once the only entrance to the deserted village.

The rutted, rocky road which once led from the highway to the bridge has long since been abandoned. Beyond the washed-out bridge, the path that ascends upward to the village is buried in the jagged remains of its crumbling desiccation.

CAMERA MOVES UP AND OVER the bridge and the long, deep gully. CAMERA PASSES OVER, AT LONG RANGE, the deserted main street of the abandoned village and on to the highest point of the plateau.

EXT.   THE HIGH PLATEAU   DAY

CAMERA ZOOMS IN to an irregular area of some five acres that is open to the sun but hidden from the wide valley we have just left. It is sheltered by violently tumbled rocks and strangely divorced from the modern world.

CAMERA MOVES IN CLOSE to examine the stony, porous soil which has been plowed and cultivated after a rude fashion in narrow, irregular strips of wheat and root vegetables such as might provide bare existence for one person. As CAMERA MOVES IN LOW along a row of fanning young wheat, it STOPS at a pair of naked, soiled feet.

CAMERA PULLS BACK and PANS UP to see the man's face as he looks downward. He has the harsh look of survival from disaster. The aura of unreality that cloaks this secretive place is also cast upon him. He peers through his narrowed eyes with the intentness of a wild animal to whom every sound and movement has significance.

A roughly trimmed beard follows the strong lines of his jaw; his long, sensual mouth is tightly folded. Except for his faded denim trousers, he is naked to the slender waist.

CONTINUED

CONTINUED

From a thin gold chain around his neck dangles a small crucifix. A pale line of protected flesh shows when the chain shifts. His weathered and embattled face is that of a boy plunged too suddenly and violently into manhood. His age is enigmatic. He is MARTIN THIBAUT.

ANOTHER ANGLE MARTIN

He crouches and strokes the shoots as one might stroke the hair of a child. Suddenly, a strong wind gusts and a CHURCH BELL from somewhere on the hillside TOLLS A CRACKED, SINGLE SOUND. It is as if Martin has heard a command. CAMERA FOLLOWS HIM as he takes a path which plunges into a shadowed ravine. At length, it joins a cobbled street.

The walls of the streets are broken, the houses deserted—windows reveal an emptiness, doors hang askew on rotted hinges. An occasional faded sign appears on a wall: an official notice of an auction, a tattered appeal to citizens to rally to their political party. In front of one of these signs, Martin stops abruptly. It is a faded, flamboyant, announcement of a circus printed on three sheets. Martin looks down at his feet.

MARTIN'S POV:

The calendar page (April 1947) lies near his foot. Also in the SHOT, the bottom of the circus poster may be seen: THE GREATEST SHOW IN PROVENCE, JUNE 24–JUNE 27, 1943.

WIDE ANGLE MARTIN

He looks up at the creaking signboard with the word: BISTRO that hangs in front of a dim, dismantled barroom. The open door and window reveal empty, cobwebbed bottles lying drunkenly askew.

ANOTHER ANGLE THE STREET

CAMERA GOES WITH MARTIN as he walks, slowly and purposefully avoiding the potholes and cobbles dislodged by the weeds and rank grass. He comes to a small church which is set back from the street. He looks up at the tower containing

CONTINUED

CONTINUED

the wrought iron, crooked belfry where the bell now hangs in silence. He enters the church.

INT. THE CHURCH DAY

The church is totally bereft. A primitive fresco on the wall has become leprous with damp. The remnants of saints and pitchforked evildoers look bleakly down from the walls. There are nail holes where the stations of the cross had hung. A confession box stands broken down under the crumbling plaster altar. Only a tall, roughly carved crucifix still hangs.

ANOTHER ANGLE THE CRUCIFIX

Martin ENTERS the SHOT. He sees one of Jesus' feet broken loose, lying half-buried in the floor's rubble. He looks at it anxiously, picks it up, blows the dust off of it, and carefully lays it on the altar. He crosses himself perfunctorily. He EXITS the SHOT.

EXT. THE CHURCH DAY

Martin ENTERS the street and follows a path around the church to its cemetery in back. The graveyard is surrounded by a low stone wall. The rusty gate groans as Martin opens and enters it.

ANOTHER ANGLE THE CEMETERY

The huddled crosses lie askew; headstones are inset with porcelain portraits of the dead: A NOTRE PERE . . . A MA FEMME CHERIE. They lean crazily in all directions, shrouded in weeds and bramble, the mounds flattened to earth level—except for one grave that lies apart in dignity. Martin goes to it.

It bears the small, firmly outlined shape of its occupant. A small orange tree casts a protective shadow over it. The green tree is neatly trimmed, and two red rose bushes are in full bloom on either side of a cross whose straightness appears austere in the midst of the others. On the cross, we can read: ANNE THIBAUT, 1890–1945. Martin kneels at the grave. He pats it gently but firmly.

CONTINUED

CONTINUED

> MARTIN
> (Quietly, as though not to
> disturb the others)
> Well, here I am, Maman.

He cocks his head a bit as though waiting for an answer.

> MARTIN (CONT'D)
> I came as fast as I could. I was busy
> weeding.
> (pause)
> The weeds are bad this year. But
> with a little rain, we should have
> good crops.

He sits for a moment in silent perplexity, his characteristi-
cally troubled eyes looking inward for some thought.

> MARTIN (CONT'D)
> Just now I found one of Christ's feet
> lying in the dust, Maman. Sometimes
> I think I hear footsteps. I run out
> into the street, but there is no one.
> I'm afraid. If there is someone about,
> he may pull down your bell . . . and
> then I shan't hear you any more.

The thought makes him cover his eyes; he sits motionless in
grief. Suddenly, he rises.

> MARTIN (CONT'D)
> I must go now, Maman. Sleep well.
> You have only to call and I shall
> hear you.

He makes the sign of the cross over her.

> MARTIN (CONT'D)
> Good day, Maman.

He turns quietly to leave. But now his sharp eyes are at-
tracted to an alien enemy. Crouching a little in his hostility,
he slinks to one side of the grave and looks down sullenly at
the ground.

CONTINUED

CONTINUED

>   MARTIN
>   Oh, it's you—hurting her. That's why
>   Maman called.

MARTIN'S POV: A THORNY PLANT

It has sprouted wildly among the roses and well-kept green-
ery of the graves.

WIDE ANGLE MARTIN AND THE PLANT

He kneels, grasps the thorny plant like a serpent, and tears
it out at the roots. Brutally, he strikes it again and again
with his fist and then crushes it in his hands, oblivious to
the pain and the blood. Yet his deep fury is not abated. He
throws the viper violently to the ground and stamps on it
madly with his bare feet. Finally, he picks up the pulp and
flings it out of the cemetery. As he wipes his bloody hands
on his trousers, he turns back to the grave.

>   MARTIN
>   Forgive me, Maman. Now he will not
>   stick you anymore. I will watch more
>   closely.

He turns sadly and EXITS the scene.

EXT. CEMETERY GATE DAY

Martin closes the gate carefully behind him and makes his
way back to the street. A HEN with a brood of tiny chicks
clucks from underneath a heap of rubble and follows at his
heels. A small BELL TINKLES in the distance, and Martin looks
OS.

MARTIN'S POV: A BARN

Through a crack in the decrepit barn door, two satanic eyes
gleam at him and a BELL SHAKES with indignation. Martin
ENTERS THE SHOT, kicks the door open, and a HERD of GOATS
seethes out. The leader charges him, butting his thigh. He
catches it by the horns, and wrestles with it in savage
playfulness. His face grows youthful with his young
laughter.

>   CONTINUED

CONTINUED

MARTIN

Old devil!

With a violent twist, the goat frees himself, and now the whole cavalcade runs past him on the cobbles as the hen and her family follow.

EXT. A GRASS-GROWN SQUARE DAY

At the end of the long main street, Martin and his companions enter the square. A low stone wall protects its flank from an abrupt descent into a winding ravine.

Martin perches himself on the wall and looks out over the near-distant washed-out-bridge and gully and the far-distant valley with its highway and opposite hills.

Behind him, the tower of the old church looms, and from its base, the village street meets the winding road that travels steeply and grotesquely down to the stone bridge whose high arch has long since collapsed in the gully below. Beyond the shattered bridge, a cart track winds brokenly to the distant highway that runs parallel with the dead village.

Swallows circle overhead, and a pigeon flutters down to rest at Martin's side.

CLOSE MARTIN'S FACE

For a moment, his brooding eyes appear to see only the serene nothingness about him. But then, slowly, we sense a growing awareness, an excitation of his animal fear. His eyes darken, and he quickly slithers off the wall to hide behind it. Slowly he rises and peers over the edge.

MARTIN'S POV: A SMALL AUTO

Still a black speck in the distance, it is careening drunkenly, suicidally along the abandoned cart road leading from the highway to the village.

EXT. CLAIRE SERRAT'S CAR (MOVING SHOT) DAY

The small, canvas-topped two-seater auto that we saw in Draguignan is being recklessly driven by Claire Serrat. Her long, black hair is flying in the wind, and we are now able to

CONTINUED

CONTINUED

SEE the faded, delicately chiseled, aristocratic face torn by a hysterical torment that is driving her to madness and to murder of herself.

CLOSE MARTIN

Swaying from side to side, like a cornered animal, he continues to peer fretfully at the car. Then he looks down at what lies below.

MARTIN'S POV: THE COLLAPSED STONE BRIDGE

Its maw beckons to the approaching auto.

BACK TO MARTIN

Confused, in a panic, he turns once again to his view of the car.

EXT. THE CAR DAY

as it hurtles wildly forward, bumping and twisting inevitably to its final destination.

INT. THE CAR DAY (OVER CLAIRE'S SHOULDER AT THE ROAD)

to SEE the washed-out bridge and the chasm beyond, as the car drifts on to its destruction.

>   CLAIRE
>   (desperate futility)
>   Robert . . . oh, Robert . . .

EXT. THE CAR (MOVING SHOT) DAY

It continues along the road, reaches the washed-out bridge, and crashes into the void and its doom in the gully below.

The accident is both massive and grotesque.

MARTIN

Confused and riveted by the catastrophe, he rises slowly from his kneeling position. After an interval, he covers his eyes with his hands, as if the sight of the accident is cracking his head.

Finally, he turns and lurches toward the church. He stops and looks up at the steeple bell as if to say, "Why don't you

CONTINUED

CONTINUED

ring?" When it doesn't, he turns back to the wall, approaching it stealthily. Once again, he peers into the gully.

MARTIN'S POV: THE CAR

It lies where it finally landed. The dust is beginning to settle. One of the wheels is still turning, glinting in the sunlight, as though beckoning to Martin.

BACK TO MARTIN

At last he slips over the wall and stumbles down the ravine to the goat track that twists its way to the edge of the deep gully. His descent into this wildly overgrown and tangled pit is long and arduous.

EXT. THE WRECKED CAR IN THE GULLY DAY

The car is perfectly still, deep in a bed of branches and stones. The canvas roof has been torn off. Martin ENTERS, clawing his way toward the car. He peers into it but sees nothing.

As he tugs at a branch, he stops abruptly and slowly looks down at his foot.

MARTIN'S POV: HIS FOOT

The toes of his bare foot are pressed against Claire's leg, which extends like a mannequin's dismembered leg from under a clump of brush. The stocking is torn away, and the naked leg obtrudes to the hip.

CU MARTIN

He stares and swallows hard, his mind wrestling with what he must do next.

Finally, CAMERA MOVES DOWN WITH MARTIN as he kneels next to the body. Cautiously, he extends his hand and places the flat of his palm on the soft thigh. As he presses, we cannot be sure if he is searching for the warmth of life or the warmth of love.

In due time, he removes his hand and reaches for a branch of the bush that covers the upper part of the body. He draws it aside, and Claire's face appears before him.

CONTINUED

CONTINUED

MED. CLOSE   CLAIRE'S FACE

It is a tattered thing of flesh and blood. Her mouth is agape
with a last, wild cry. At that precise moment, she takes a
broken, dying breath which startles Martin, causing him to
draw back and release the branch.

PHOTO EFFECT:

As the leafy frond quivers back to its original position in
front of Claire's face, CAMERA MOVES IN ON THE IMAGE OF
SHIMMERING LEAVES WHICH THEN BLENDS INTO A DIFFUSED FOCUS OF

CU   CLAIRE SERRAT'S HAIR

It is shaking and shimmering in the photographic DISSOLVE as
CAMERA PULLS BACK to reveal Claire looking at herself in a
mirror. She is combing her shoulder-length black hair, while
seated in front of a dressing table. Behind her is a screen
which might be found in a doctor's office to effect a degree
of privacy. In fact, that's precisely what it is—a section of
DR. JOHN FENWICK's office in England that serves as his
dressing room.

CLOSE   CLAIRE IN THE MIRROR

It is the young, dead-white face of a girl of 24 without
makeup. Now, in repose, we can see clearly the drawn, wan,
and sickly look of a tragic disease which has caused deep
hollows under the brilliant, incandescent blue eyes and
straight black brows. There is a misty dust on the mirror,
which does not help matters.

She finishes, puts the comb in her expensive alligator bag,
and rises out of the SHOT.

INT.   DR. FENWICK'S OFFICE   DAY

As Claire ENTERS from behind the screen, we can see Dr.
Fenwick standing at the window. We can also detect that he
is actually lost in his own thoughts. He is an old man, weary
and stoop-shouldered, and his deep-lined face is grim behind
his spectacles. The office is shabby, with an atmosphere of
despair and disorder. There is a desk, in the center of which
we SEE several X-RAY SQUARES OF CELLULOID.

CONTINUED

CONTINUED

CLAIRE

ENTERS, trying to zip up the back of her dress. She looks toward Fenwick.

DR. FENWICK

CAMERA is ANGLED ACROSS HIS BACK to look out the window. We see a neglected, rain-drenched garden. Beyond the ill-trimmed hedges—shrouded in a driving mist—are the Kentish Wolds.

> CLAIRE'S VOICE (OS)
> I can't reach the damn thing. Please
> do me up.

She approaches and gives him her back. Fenwick looks displeased as he tugs viciously at the zipper of her expensive black dress and is finally successful.

> FENWICK
> What do you think I am? One of
> your gigolos?

Claire smiles in a characteristic attitude of detachment, with no self-pity. She walks to the desk and sits in front of it. She takes out a cigarette and lights it, inhaling deeply. As Fenwick sits opposite her, he shakes his head in obvious distress. With unsteady hands, he picks up the X-ray sheets and throws them roughly down again.

> FENWICK
> Why do you bring me all this tripe?
> (irritably)
> I'm an out-of-date country doctor
> passing my last days here in Serrat
> County . . . and besides, I drink too
> much. Why don't you accept the
> diagnosis and advice of your Harley
> Street high-mucky-muck doctors.

> CLAIRE
> They've run out of advice. The ghost
> is catching up with me. You brought
> (MORE)

CONTINUED

CONTINUED

> CLAIRE (CONT'D)
> me into the world; it seems fitting
> that you should see me out of it.

> FENWICK
> Don't talk like a damn fool. It's not
> that bad. All the same, you're obvi-
> ously trying to kill yourself. I'd like
> to know why.

Claire has her answer. She rises and crosses to the window.

> FENWICK (CONT'D)
> Why? Why? You were such a
> charming child—such a lovely, gra-
> cious girl. You come of fine stock.
> Your father and mother were the salt
> of our good earth.

> CLAIRE
> Pity that good earth had to crumble.
> Perhaps I came here to be reminded
> of the contempt I have for myself.

> FENWICK
> Then why don't you do something
> about it. You look dissipated! You
> *are* dissipated. You excuse yourself, I
> suppose, like all of your generation,
> with your disinheritance. Well, we
> are all disinherited in one way or
> another. You make me sick!

> CLAIRE
> (with compassion)
> Just as you so often made me well.

She looks out of the window at the pouring rain, and beyond.

EXT. CLAIRE'S POV DAY

At first, we see the same garden and the wolds that Fenwick
saw. Then, gradually, within the wolds, the mist clears a
little and a picture materializes. It is the charred and

CONTINUED

CONTINUED

burned-out remnants of a castle. Barely more than the foundation and fragments of the framework exist. Elsewhere the ground is covered with the rubble that was once Serrat Manor. Although it is not raining here, the picture is subdued by a misty gloom.

INT. DR. FENWICK'S OFFICE DAY

ANGLE CLAIRE AT THE WINDOW

As she stares, sightlessly, a LOW, DRONING SOUND begins to be HEARD OS. The SOUND INCREASES until we can identify it as the approach of airplanes. Claire looks upward into the sky.

EXT. SKY NIGHT (CLAIRE'S POV)

Slowly, out of the darkness, we discern a squadron of bombers coming toward us. Soon, the Nazi swastikas on the planes are visible. A moment later, the airplanes commence to unload their bombs. As the bombs hurtle to the ground, CAMERA PANS DOWN to SEE a LONG SHOT of the castle before its destruction. All about it, bombs explode, shattering the countryside.

INT. SERRAT MANOR (THE LIBRARY) NIGHT

It is heavily curtained. The prideful possessions normally found in such a room are fading and breaking under the load of warfare. The Chinese Chippendale wallpaper has begun to peel and carry the stains of the deadly creeping sickness.

In a corner of the library are three beds, side by side. CAMERA MOVES IN on them. Claire, now 17, is in her nightclothes, sitting up in bed, fearstruck by the awful detonations. NANNY-ANNE, the governess since Claire's infancy, sits in her nightclothes next to Claire and holds her close.

> NANNY-ANNE
> Don't worry, Monkey, it will soon be
> over.

> CLAIRE
> I'm sure I'd feel better in my own
> bedroom, Nanny-Anne.

CONTINUED

CONTINUED

> NANNY-ANNE
>
> I'm sure. But short of a direct hit,
> the library is safest. After all, His
> Lordship's judgment is best.

> CLAIRE
>
> When will it end?

> NANNY-ANNE
>
> Soon, Monkey. It takes more than a
> German clown to destroy us.

WIDE ANGLE THE DOOR TO THE LIBRARY

It opens and three people ENTER. The first is LADY MARY
SERRAT, a well-preserved lady in her fifties. She is followed
by a youthful FLIGHT COMMANDER in uniform. The last to
enter is SIR CLAUD SERRAT. He wears a military uniform and
insignia of a colonel. He leads the other two across the room
to a desk which stands in front of a terrace window with
double doors in the center. The window, like all the others,
is heavily draped. All three people demonstrate a calm
discipline. As Serrat crosses to his desk . . .

> SERRAT
> (to Claire and Nanny-Anne)
>
> Sorry.
> (to the Commander)
> I'm quite sure I have the list of
> Everett's possessions here.

He begins to look through the drawers.

> LADY MARY
>
> It was most kind of you, Com-
> mander, when you must be so hard-
> pressed.

Serrat finds the envelope.

> SERRAT
>
> Ah, here it is.

He hands the envelope to the Commander.

CONTINUED

CONTINUED

> COMMANDER
> Thank you, Sir. He was a great
> fighter, you know—a fine officer—
> much loved. You should be proud.

> SERRAT
> We are. Thank you again.

> COMMANDER
> I'll call you—very soon.

> LADY SERRAT
> Goodbye, Commander.

> COMMANDER
> Goodbye, Lady Mary. Colonel.

With a slight bow, he turns and EXITS the room. Lord and
Lady Serrat stand silently looking at one another.

ANGLE   CLAIRE AND NANNY-ANNE

Claire, silent, astonished, stares at her parents. Slowly, she
gets out of bed. GO WITH HER as she crosses the room to her
parents.

> CLAIRE
> (to her father)
> Is it Everett?
> (Serrat doesn't answer)
> Father?

As Serrat turns to his daughter, only his eyes convey his
great, deep-seated anguish.

> SERRAT
> Your brother has served his country,
> Claire.

Claire continues to stare silently; the shock is enormous.
Finally, Serrat loses his control.

> SERRAT
> Do you want to see him?

Emphatic now, he turns and crosses to the window. He
draws back the curtains and flings open the terrace doors.

CONTINUED

CONTINUED

> LADY MARY
> (consternated)
> Claud, what are you doing?

> SERRAT
> (to Claire)
> Come here, then.

Claire crosses to her father. He takes her hand and leads her outside. Lady Mary follows them.

> LADY MARY
> Claud, please!

EXT. TERRACE NIGHT

The planes are still droning overhead; the ground quivers under the occasional blasts. Lord Serrat points to the sky.

> SERRAT
> See. Everett is up there. But he's
> safe now—safe.

> LADY MARY
> Come in, for God's sake! It does no
> one any good to take such risks.

> SERRAT
> (with a strange rage and
> exaltation)
> She must see and remember. This is
> one of the great battles of the world.

Claire begins to cough convulsively.

> LADY MARY
> Now see what you've done. You
> know how easily she catches cold.
> This could be the death of her.

> SERRAT
> But she must look. Look! We're all
> of us giving our lives for it.

MOVE IN ON CLAIRE'S FACE as she continues to cough convulsively.

LAP DISSOLVE TO:

INT. FENWICK'S OFFICE   DAY

ON CLAIRE'S BACK

She is facing the window and coughing convulsively. Fenwick ENTERS the SHOT. He holds out a small glass of medicine. Claire turns around.

> FENWICK
> I've told you before, and I tell you
> again: as long as you will it, you'll
> cough.
> > (hands her the glass)
> Drink this.

With great effort, Claire swallows the drink. The cough begins to subside. Fenwick takes her arm and leads her back to the chair. He returns to his chair and waits for her to recover. Finally, Claire places her hands on the desk in a gesture of surrender. She smiles weakly.

> CLAIRE
> All right, I'll be good. I'll do what I'm
> told. What are the doctor's orders?
> Fresh air, good food, and virtuous—if
> not laborious—days?

> FENWICK
> > (cynically)
> Can you afford them?

> CLAIRE
> Don't you recognize a Dior creation?
> I'm a very well-kept woman.

Fenwick stands up. Violently, he seizes the X-ray films and dashes them to the floor.

> FENWICK
> Get out of here, you damned little
> city tramp!

He turns his back to her to control his temper. Claire rises. She crosses to a nearby chair and picks up her coat. Fenwick comes to her; he takes it out of her hands.

CONTINUED

CONTINUED

> FENWICK
> (scowling)
> Let me help you.
> (then)
> I'll see you to your car.

He leads the way to the door. Claire EXITS, he FOLLOWS.

EXT. DR. FENWICK'S HOME   DAY

ANGLE INCLUDES the little two-seater roadster with the canvas top parked at the curb.

MED. SHOT   THE ENTRANCE DOOR

Fenwick looks up at the RAIN, then at Claire. His scowl turns to shamefaced affection.

> FENWICK
> You mustn't get those absurd feet
> wet.

With astonishing strength, he lifts her into his arms. PAN with him as he lurches through the rain to the car, wrenches the door open, and dumps Claire onto the seat. He slams the door shut, and leans into the window opening.

> FENWICK
> (panting)
> I'm still man enough to handle a
> good-for-nothing wench like you.

Now, as they look at each other warmly, the rain runs down Fenwick's stubbled cheeks as though he might be crying.

> FENWICK
> (tenderly)
> Remember, you're all I have left of
> our good days. Child—don't leave me
> destitute. Live for me.

> CLAIRE
> (murmurs)
> I'll try. I promise.

She leans forward and kisses his cheek gently.

CONTINUED

CONTINUED

> FENWICK
> Where are you going now?

> CLAIRE
> Gather my thoughts first. Then—I
> know a small hotel in Draguignan.

> FENWICK
> Draguignan? That's the south of
> France, isn't it? Excellent place.

> CLAIRE
> (ruminating)
> Once—it was blissful.

WIDE ANGLE   THE CAR

Fenwick stands erect; the car moves out. He watches mournfully in the rain as it leaves.

INT.   THE CAR   (MOVING SHOT)   (RAIN)   DAY

CAMERA MOVES IN on CLAIRE until her face fills the frame.

> CLAIRE
> To say goodbye—to live—or not to
> live . . .

Her eyes brim with tears. She stares sightlessly at the road ahead.

CLAIRE'S POV: A NAMELESS STREET   NIGHT

The rain has stopped; the windshield wipers are still.

The street is run-down, dirty, and disorderly, lined with cheap tenement flats and common stores. The gloom lights the narrow sidewalks. The car comes to a stop at the curb. At the far end of the street we can SEE a marquee of a decrepit, small theater. The dreary sign READS: KINGS ROAD THEATRE, and underneath, in smaller letters: CHELSEA.

CLOSE   CLAIRE

She leans across the steering wheel and looks upward through the windshield at one of the tenement windows.

EXT. A SMALL BUILDING (CLAIRE'S POV) NIGHT

It is a sleazy affair. CAMERA ANGLE is UPWARD toward one of
its windows. A girl seems to be standing there, looking down
at us. CAMERA ZOOMS IN SLOWLY until we can see very clearly
that it is CLAIRE. Her face is drawn, wan, and sickly pale,
but the hollows are not as deep, and we can now clearly SEE
the contours of her patrician beauty.

INT. CLAIRE'S ROOM NIGHT

It is a scrubby one-room flat. From somewhere above, we
HEAR the SOUND OF MUSIC. At first, the strange high pitch
gives it a weird flavor. But, as it becomes more discernible,
we recognize it as the recording of a European vocalist being
played on a cheap gramophone.

The room itself is misshapen and poorly furnished. Two
seedy lamps provide the light. A makeshift highboy chest
stands in a corner, and next to it is a disreputable-looking
table with an ordinary purse lying open on it. The tiny room
has a single window and one door which leads to the hall. In
addition to a bed in the corner, a few other pieces of dilapidated furniture are scattered around.

Claire, wearing a flimsy nightgown, has just left the window
and is crossing to the table upon which her purse lies. She
takes out a cigarette, lights it, and inhales deeply. She
glances appreciatively at the ceiling as the music plays.

The raw chill of the room is too much for her in the flimsy
nightgown, so she crosses to the highboy, takes out a robe,
and puts it on. THERE IS A KNOCK AT THE DOOR. Claire reacts
with a start, then opens the door to find Lord Serrat. He is
carrying an overnight bag as he ENTERS.

> CLAIRE
>
> Father . . .

> SERRAT
>
> I've brought you something.

As Claire snuffs out her cigarette in an ashtray full of dead
butts, he opens the bag and removes several Wedgwood
pieces, each encrusted with a coat of arms, and two beautiful, tall silver candlesticks. Claire joins him as he sits.

CONTINUED

CONTINUED

> SERRAT
> We've no further use for these. They
> should bring a fair price.

> CLAIRE
> But all these things belong in the
> manor.

> SERRAT
> The manor is closed, child—empty
> for the first time in its history.

Claire is speechless.

> SERRAT (CONT'D)
> You should have known it would
> happen. Sit down, Claire.

They both sit.

> CLAIRE
> (still profoundly shocked)
> But where do you live?

> SERRAT
> (dismissing it lightly)
> There are other homes besides
> Serrat.

> CLAIRE
> But, it isn't fair . . .

> SERRAT
> Fairness isn't the point, child. It's
> just that—well, I'm afraid our kind is
> finished. Perhaps we weren't fitted
> to survive—though it seems we were
> a useful lot—dependable, you know,
> with decent standards. But, I sup-
> pose standards are out of date.

> CLAIRE
> What shall you do?

CONTINUED

CONTINUED

> SERRAT
> That isn't why I came. It's you,
> Claire.
> (earnestly)
> You have to start out on a new road,
> child. Strike new roots. You have one
> asset: yourself. You've brains and
> good looks. God knows, you didn't get
> your looks from me, and they're not
> your mother's kind either. You hark
> back to great-great-grandmother
> Mathilda. Do you remember her
> portrait? A raving beauty. We
> thought it was a Vandyke, but it
> wasn't. So it didn't help much.

Claire has hardly heard him. Suddenly, from above, the
pleasant gramophone music is cut short, and a moment
later, it is replaced with a vigorous fox-trot. SIMULT, a COUPLE
starts to dance vigorously until the ceiling begins to shake
and creak. Serrat becomes abruptly impatient. He rises.

> SERRAT
> This is scarcely a place to discuss
> such things.

He crosses to the door, Claire following.

> SERRAT (CONT'D)
> Your mother will be in touch with
> you, I'm sure.

With an erratic mood swing, he becomes saddened,
depressed.

> SERRAT (CONT'D)
> Forgive me, child.

He leaves. Claire stands, forlornly thoughtful. But, in the
next moment, she is distracted by the SOUND of a DOOR OVER-
HEAD BURSTING OPEN, and FOOTSTEPS RACING DOWN THE STAIRS.
Hard upon this, there is a frantic KNOCK on her DOOR.

CONTINUED

CONTINUED

Claire stands for a moment, distrustful. The KNOCK IS RE-
PEATED WITH A FAMILIAR RHYTHM: SHAVE AND A HAIRCUT, SHAM-
POO. Claire smiles.

ANGLE THE DOOR (ACROSS CLAIRE'S SHOULDER)

Claire opens it, and ROBERT is there. His eyes blaze with a
delightfully exciting passion. Even with the sordid staircase
and the naked overhanging electric bulb behind him, Robert
shines with his own light. He manages, in shirtsleeves, to be
extremely elegant.

> ROBERT
> (brightly)
> Our so-called landlady—God knows
> she's no lady—told me about you.

REVERSE ACROSS ROBERT'S SHOULDER TO CLAIRE

Claire is clearly grateful for his intrusion.

> ROBERT
> And I thought we might have a drink
> together.

> CLAIRE
> (drawing her robe tighter)
> I don't think I'm . . .

REVERSE ROBERT

> ROBERT
> My name's Robert Allwyn. Real
> name Binns—better forgotten. I'm an
> actor.

REVERSE CLAIRE

She laughs good-naturedly.

> ROBERT'S VOICE (OS)
> What's your line?

> CLAIRE
> My line? I haven't got one. But I
> suppose I'll have to find one soon.

CONTINUED

CONTINUED

TWO SHOT (FAVORING ROBERT)

>ROBERT
>If you mean that you're broke, you
>couldn't be in more congenial com-
>pany.

His confidence will not brook Claire's uncertainty. He
reaches for her hand and takes it.

>ROBERT (CONT'D)
>Well, come along.

Claire laughs at his cocksureness. She follows him.

INT. STAIRWELL NIGHT

>ROBERT
>By the way—Candy and I are living
>in sin. Hope you don't mind.

>CLAIRE
>I don't mind anything, so long as
>you're alive.

INT. CANDY'S ROOM NIGHT

It contains battered, undusted furniture, a clutter of un-
washed dishes, empty bottles stacked by a blazing fireside, a
double bed, unmade, in the center of this disorder. CANDY,
thirtyish, a Yorkshire terrier with a yellow fringe hanging
over amber eyes, is toasting a bun as Robert and Claire
ENTER.

>CANDY
>Hello there. So glad you've come.
>Robert and I are fit to be tied, we're
>so sick of each other.

She searches noisily among the bottles.

>CANDY (CONT'D)
>I hope you can stomach gin and lime.
>It seems to be all we've got left.

>CLAIRE
>I'll try anything once.

CONTINUED

CONTINUED

Robert leads Claire to a chair by the fire. He offers her a cigarette, and lights it for her.

> ROBERT
> Lovely, isn't she, Candy? But a bit
> on the skimpy side. Those shadows
> and hollows are damned attractive,
> but you shouldn't overdo them. I
> prescribe a course of juicy steaks
> and rude belly laughs.

> CANDY
> Harken to the melting voice. He's an
> actor—a bit on the hammy side.

> ROBERT
> (unruffled)
> Candy talks rot by rote.

> CANDY
> You've already sampled his will of
> iron. Wait till he gets into top gear.
> You won't have a bitch's chance—if
> you'll excuse my coarseness.

Robert becomes grave, as if shouldering Candy out of their presence.

> ROBERT
> What can you do?

> CLAIRE
> (ruefully)
> I dance well. I speak French and
> German.

> ROBERT
> Good French?

> CLAIRE
> The best.

> CANDY
> He's got his teeth into you. But
> you've still got time to make a run
> for it.

CONTINUED

CONTINUED

> ROBERT
> See how hog-tied she is?

He sits on a stool at Claire's feet, leaning toward her.

> ROBERT (CONT'D)
> Sounds like we're answers to each
> other's prayers. I go into rehearsal
> in the starring role of a new play.
> Our producer is looking for a French
> maid. Two lines ending with "ooh la
> la!" Think you could manage that?

> CLAIRE
> I could make a big try.

> ROBERT
> That's my girl.

He quickly draws Claire to her feet in front of him.

> ROBERT (CONT'D)
> All right. Now—talk French.

> CLAIRE
> Je vous remercie, Monsieur,
> infiniment.

> ROBERT
> Sounds good to me. Now, say "ooh la
> la!"

> CLAIRE
> (much too solemnly)
> Ooh la la.

They all laugh. He takes her in his arms.

> ROBERT
> Now—dance.

CAMERA RISES to an OVERHEAD SHOT

With his abundant energy, Robert begins to pivot her round
and round in circles . . .

LAP DISSOLVE:

CONTINUED

CONTINUED

PROCESS SHOT

A PLATE of the panoramic view of Draguignan as it was seen in the MAIN TITLE is spinning round and round. It comes to a STOP.

EXT.   LONG SHOT   DRAGUIGNAN   DAY

We PICK UP the two-seater car threading its way through the town. This time, we FOLLOW IT more closely as it proceeds to the hotel.

EXT.   THE HOTEL IN DRAGUIGNAN   DAY

The car stops in front of the hotel, and Claire gets out. This time we can identify her as she enters the hotel.

INT. HOTEL DINING ROOM   DAY

ANGLE from the back of the room to INCLUDE the EIGHT TABLES of the small dining room, as well as the hotel entrance foyer with its CASHIER'S DESK and small adjacent OFFICE in BG. Next to this office is an uncarpeted stairway that leads to the rooms above. Behind the desk sits a stout, black-clad PATRONNE.

IN CAMERA FG are FOUR LUSTY OLD MEN, their napkins anchored to their collars. Three of them are vigorous, handsome natives of Provence with Rembrandtesque faces. They are themselves artists. The FOURTH MAN is different: a Northern intellectual who wears neat city clothes, a pince-nez, and a pointed gray beard.

Claire is seated at a table in the BG, nearest the foyer. She wears a different dress and is fingering a glass of wine. GEORGES, a garçon-à-tout-faire, is approaching the table of the four men with a trayful of food. The FOURTH MAN, with an air of academic authority, is holding forth.

> FOURTH MAN
> At heart, a country depends for its
> greatness not on her industries but
> on her fields. A healthy, vigorous
> rural population is the only hope for
> France and her survival.

CONTINUED

CONTINUED

The other three start eating immediately. It is obvious, however, that the FIRST MAN is their spokesman. He has a large, humorous face with big, bushy eyebrows crowning his continually dancing, animated eyes.

> FIRST MAN
> And that is why the ministry has sent you on this voyage of rediscovery?

> FOURTH MAN
> It is my task to seek out old historic villages that lie to the north of Draguignan—villages that have been deserted by a discouraged population—and see what can be done to pour new life into them.

> FIRST MAN
> And we are to help you choose those villages?

He looks up, and his humorous eye meets Claire's.

CLAIRE (FIRST MAN'S POV)

Abashed at being part of their conversation, she lights a cigarette and inhales deeply. As she fingers her glass of red wine, she looks much as she did when she left Dr. Fenwick's office. OVER THIS:

> FOURTH MAN'S
> VOICE (OS)
> Yes. You are all Provençals and well-regarded artists whose advice the Beaux Arts will respect. You, above all, will know what is worthy of restoration.

FIRST MAN (TO INCLUDE CLAIRE)

> FIRST MAN
> (sniffs)
> What is worthy of restoration. A wise man sheds himself periodically
> (MORE)

CONTINUED

CONTINUED

>   FIRST MAN (CONT'D)
>   as a snake sheds his skin. He leaves
>   what he was behind him and forgets
>   what is useless to remember.

He casts an impish glance at Claire. The moment is uncomfortable for her, and she averts his glance. Suddenly, there is the tearing cough. Once again, she is unable to control the convulsive spasm.

FULL SHOT   THE DINING ROOM

With all eyes focused on her, Claire manages to rise and hurry from the room.

ANGLE   THE CASHIER'S DESK   THE PATRONNE

Her glowering eyes follow Claire as she hurries past the desk and onward up the steep stairway. Georges ENTERS the SHOT. He leans on the desk, looking after Claire.

>   GEORGES
>   Poor girl.

>   PATRONNE
>   (resentful)
>   Poor girl!

>   GEORGES
>   You know her?

>   PATRONNE
>   She has been here before. We do not
>   complain if she comes with her
>   lover. But all night they would keep
>   the clients awake—laughing, singing,
>   drinking . . .

Georges shrugs tolerantly.

>   PATRONNE (CONT'D)
>   And now, again, she disturbs them.
>   A client has complained that she
>   coughed all night.

>   GEORGES
>   Une poule.

                                          CONTINUED

> PATRONNE
> She can cough her lungs out some-
> where else. We have consideration
> for our clients.

A BUZZER is HEARD. The Patronne and Georges look OS.

POV: WHAT THEY SEE

AN INDICATOR BOX on the wall showing room 8.

PREVIOUS SCENE

> GEORGES
> I will see what she wants.

Georges starts up the stairway.

INT. THE FIRST LANDING DAY

CAMERA PANS WITH GEORGES as he reaches the floor and proceeds down the hall to room 8. He knocks, opens the door,
and EXITS into the room.

INT. ROOM 8 DAY

It is typically appointed. Claire is putting one last item in
her battered suitcase as Georges enters.

> CLAIRE
> You can tell Madam that I'm leaving.

She snaps the suitcase shut.

> GEORGES
> Oui, Mam'selle.

> CLAIRE
> The car, please.

Georges takes the valise.

> GEORGES
> Oui, Mam'selle.

He opens the door and exits. Claire follows.

EXT. THE HIGHWAY DAY

Claire's car is seen as it speeds along the familiar highway
that we saw in our opening scenes.

CONTINUED

CONTINUED

CLAIRE'S CAR   MOVING SHOT

OVER THE SHOULDER OF CLAIRE   (THROUGH THE WINDSHIELD)

On the hood of the car as it speeds along, the vision of Robert materializes. His clear figure is translucent in the daylight so that we can see the trees and roadside scenery passing through him. He is exhilarated and full of excitement.

>   ROBERT
>   I've nailed it, my sweet!

>   CLAIRE'S VOICE (OS)
>   (ecstatic)
>   Oh, my darling darling—

REVERSE SHOT   CLAIRE

>   CLAIRE
>   Robert, don't leave me . . .

Claire cries pitifully, and soon begins to cough. She raises a handkerchief to her mouth, and when she takes it away, it is stained red. Suddenly, something through the windshield catches her eye.

EXT.   CLAIRE'S POV: A SIGNPOST   DAY

It is simply a faded board propped casually against a stone: It reads: ROUTE BARRE. ROAD CLOSED. The signpost points drunkenly away from the valley, seemingly at nothing. Now, through the windshield, we see the car slowing down. It comes to a stop at the side of the road.

BACK TO CLAIRE

>   CLAIRE
>   Darling . . . how could I tell you what
>   was wrong? How could I stand in
>   your way? How could I explain what
>   I have to do?

With a determined glint, she puts the car in gear and shoots forward.

EXT. THE CAR DAY

The little car wheels crazily onto the deserted cart track, then wildly forward along the narrow, rutted, winding ascent.

CAMERA MOVES IN ON THE REAR WHEEL UNTIL THE SPINNING MOTION FILLS THE FRAME.

LAP DISSOLVE:

INT. OVERHEAD SHOT MARTIN'S ROOM DAY

as Claire's spinning face comes to a stop. She turns her face from side to side as she writhes in pain. The blood of the accident has been washed off her face, but she still has deep cuts, gashes, and bruises on her neck, shoulders, and arms. Her lips are thickly swollen. Her hair has been roughly cropped very short. Her eyes, when she opens them, are fevered and half alive.

CAMERA PULLS BACK to reveal Claire lying on an old, tattered bed. There is no pillow; she is covered with a coarse, gray sheet. A window which is no more than a small opening in the wall is next to the bed. It is covered grotesquely with a broken-slatted shutter. The room is lighted by thin shafts of sun that peer through the slats into the semidarkness. CAMERA HOLDS when the ANGLE is wide enough to INCLUDE Claire's body. Within the pools of light, we can see enough to know that Claire lies naked under the sheet: her bare shoulders show at the top; her naked feet and ankles show at the bottom. Her delirious eyes rove from the window to the ceiling.

CLAIRE'S POV: THE CEILING

It is low, broken, and weirdly patched. Shadows from the fluttering leaves of the tree outside the window play there like goblins. The eerie picture is slightly out of focus to match Claire's fever. CAMERA PANS slightly down the wall and HOLDS abruptly to FRAME MARTIN'S HEAD AND CHEST. He stands in a pale patch of sunlight.

CU CLAIRE

Stares in hypnotic fascination.

CONTINUED

CONTINUED

ANGLE MARTIN (AS BEFORE)

Slowly, CAMERA FOCUS is CORRECTED.

Martin, half naked, looks monstrous. His brilliant, visionary stare fixed motionlessly on Claire adds a mood of savagery. CAMERA PANS DOWN to his feet, bare and soiled on the earthen floor.

CLOSE CLAIRE

Unable any longer to stand the sight of Martin, she closes her fevered eyes.

> CLAIRE
> (whimpers)
> Nanny-Anne—please come—it
> hurts—it hurts so . . .

Martin ENTERS the SHOT. He has a metal cup in his hand which he holds out toward her. Wary and uncertain, he puts the cup to her lips.

> MARTIN
> Drink.

Claire's lips are stiff and unresponsive. Her eyes are still closed; she jerks her head away.

> MARTIN (CONT'D)
> (timidly)
> You must drink, Mademoiselle.

Claire does not move. Suddenly, with more firmness than anger, Martin seizes her head and forces the liquid into her throat. This done, he smiles, feeling surer of himself.

He secures a faded, rough pillow and places it under her head. He pushes open the shutters, letting the sun in, and LIGHTING THE ROOM. Then he kneels on the floor near Claire's head and waits silently, as a child would.

Claire stares secretly at the expressionless intensity of a stranger who, with some slight or incautious movement, might become a dangerous enemy.

CONTINUED

CONTINUED

> CLAIRE
> (weakly)
> Who are you?

> MARTIN
> (low-pitched, as though to
> match the weakness of
> Claire)
> Martin. Martin Thibaut.

> CLAIRE
> What is this?

> MARTIN
> My house.

> CLAIRE
> How did I get here?

> MARTIN
> (with pride, pointing to
> himself)
> Me. You did not see that the bridge
> was down.

> CLAIRE
> You . . . why didn't you leave me?

> MARTIN
> You were bleeding badly.

Martin thinks hard, then asks mysteriously,

> MARTIN
> Did you want to kill yourself?

> CLAIRE
> (sobs)
> Yes.

> MARTIN
> (sadly)
> That is too bad. You have only hurt
> yourself.

CONTINUED

CONTINUED

> CLAIRE
> (bewildered)
> How badly?

> MARTIN
> (shrugs)
> I don't know.

> CLAIRE
> But what did the doctor say?

> MARTIN
> (puzzled)
> Doctor? There is no doctor.

Claire frowns. Though fearful of Martin's strangeness, she is emboldened by her hysteria.

> CLAIRE
> But you must have sent for one . . .

Martin continues to look puzzled.

> CLAIRE (CONT'D)
> Don't you understand me?

> MARTIN
> (explaining)
> My mother and I live here alone.

Claire feels a momentary illusion of comfort. She whispers like a sick child.

> CLAIRE
> My face—it feels strange—hard and
> stiff.

> MARTIN
> Oh, those are the cuts. Some were
> very deep. But they are better now.
> Maybe one day they will just be
> white lines to remind you . . .

> CLAIRE
> Of what?

CONTINUED

CONTINUED

>   MARTIN
>   (shrugs)
> That one does not die easily.

Disturbed by the significance of this remark, Claire lifts a shaking hand to her hair.

>   CLAIRE
>   (realizing)
> My hair—it's gone!

>   MARTIN
> I could not manage all that bloody
> mess. I had to cut it.

Claire covers her eyes and cries.

>   CLAIRE
> What have you done?
>   (when she recovers)
> How long have I been here?

>   MARTIN
> The apple tree was in bud when I
> carried you here.
>   (he smiles)
> It is in bloom now.

In shock, Claire tries to rise. Feebly, painfully, her arms and torso obey her, but her legs are dead. She looks at her feet.

CLAIRE'S POV: HER FEET

Motionless, they extend from beneath the coarse sheet.

>   CLAIRE
> My legs—I can't move them.

Once again, she struggles to move them. To no avail.

>   MARTIN
> It may be that your back is hurt. It
> may mend, too. When I was little, I
> had a dog who was hurt in a fight.
>   (oddly animated)
>   (MORE)

                                        CONTINUED

CONTINUED

> MARTIN (CONT'D)
> For a long time she dragged her back
> legs. Papa wanted to knock her
> brains out. But I cried. In time, her
> strength came back. She could even
> help to guard our sheep.
> > (moralizing)
> One must have patience.

> CLAIRE
> > (in frantic despair)
> Patience!

Claire emits a strange, cackling laugh. It unnerves Martin.
He runs his hand through his hair in bafflement as Claire is
suddenly seized with a paroxysm. The cough tears at her
wounds so that, even with her teeth set in furious pride, she
groans. Finally, the coughing abates, and she tastes the
familiar deadly sweetness. She puts a corner of the coarse
sheet to her mouth, and when she takes it away, we see a
bright red stain on the cloth. With a flourish of ironic relief,
she shows it to Martin.

> CLAIRE
> There . . . you see . . . I'm going to
> die soon anyway.

> MARTIN
> > (solemnly)
> Maman says, "That is as God wills."

At the name "Maman" the illusory comfort returns to Claire.

> CLAIRE
> Tell your Maman I want to see her.
> Now.

Martin looks beyond Claire at some secret vision.

> MARTIN
> She does not come here anymore.

> CLAIRE
> Why not?

CONTINUED

CONTINUED

> MARTIN
> She lives in our cemetery.

> CLAIRE
> (horrified)
> You mean . . . she's dead?

Martin, disconcerted, rises. He picks up the cup and crosses to the opposite wall where he places the cup on a dilapidated cupboard. He stands with his face to the wall.

> MARTIN
> Maman is very tired. She has had a
> hard life. It was time for her to rest.
> But she always wakes and listens
> when I talk to her. She told me what
> to do for you. She said: "God has
> sent her to you, Martin. Be careful
> and patient with her."

Claire closes her eyes in sick consternation. Martin returns and sits on the edge of the bed facing her . . . waiting until she is goaded to look up at him.

> CLAIRE
> Have you taken care of me—alone?

> MARTIN
> (obviously)
> There is no one else. Besides, I'm
> used to sick people and animals.
> They are much the same.
> (smiles)
> Except people complain more. Ani-
> mals know that one does one's best. I
> have Maman's herbs. They ease
> pain. They made you sleep.

> CLAIRE
> (incredulous)
> What about my people? Didn't it
> occur to you that they might be
> looking for me?

CONTINUED

CONTINUED

                        MARTIN
                     (shrewdly)
             You have no people.

                        CLAIRE
             How do you know?

                        MARTIN
             There was nothing but your
             passport.
                     (conspiratorially)
             I thought, "She, too, does not want to
             be found."

                        CLAIRE
                     (now childishly wheedling)
             I can see you're a good man. I'm
             sure you realize that without help I
             may be crippled for life.

                        MARTIN
                     (artfully)
             If you are going to die, Mademoiselle,
             does that matter?

                        CLAIRE
                     (weakly but furiously)
             At least I have a right to die where I
             choose—among civilized people!
             What you're doing is an abominably
             cruel thing.
                     (slyly, now)
             Your mother must be a good woman.
             Ask her what you should do.

                        MARTIN
             She warned me. She said, "Don't let
             her betray you, Martin."

                        CLAIRE
             Betray! What is there to betray?!
                     (then)
             You said you didn't want to be found.
             What have you done?

                                        CONTINUED

CONTINUED

Martin's body stiffens.

>   CLAIRE
>   (cautiously)
>   Are you hiding?

INSERT   MARTIN'S HANDS

They are so tightly splayed on his thighs that they look
bloodless.

CLOSE   CLAIRE

>   CLAIRE
>   (same)
>   What are you hiding from?

>   MARTIN
>   (tensely)
>   Mademoiselle, I did not ask you to
>   come here. I do not ask you ques-
>   tions. I do not have to answer yours.

TWO SHOT   MARTIN AND CLAIRE

>   CLAIRE
>   (mounting panic)
>   But you're running a great risk. If I
>   die on your hands . . .

>   MARTIN
>   (roughly)
>   No one would know.
>   (satisfied, his tension eases)
>   Our cemetery is crowded. But I would
>   find a place for you—next to Maman.
>   She is a quiet woman. She would not
>   trouble you.

He rises and crosses to the cupboard; he pours a liquid into
the metal cup.

>   MARTIN
>   You are a foreigner. You have
>   nowhere to go—no one to turn to—or
>   you would tell me.

                              CONTINUED

CONTINUED

He crosses back to the bed with the cup in his hand.

> MARTIN (CONT'D)
> Drink this. It is good goat's milk. It
> will give you strength.

As he tries to hold her head again, she pushes the cup out of
his hands and then, as suddenly, goes limp. Once more, her
mind begins to cloud. This time, added to the fever, agony
and humiliation arise from the fact of her immediate, very
personal need.

> CLAIRE
> (whimpers feverishly)
> Please, Nanny-Anne . . . please come.
> If you don't, I won't be able to help
> myself, and then you'll scold me. But
> it won't be my fault.

CLOSE   MARTIN

His expression indicates that he senses her need.

BACK TO SCENE

Martin crosses to the cupboard and selects an object, a flat
pan. He returns to Claire and removes the sheet from the
lower half of her body. He raises her hips and slides the
object underneath her.

In the next moment, as her semidelirium clears, she lays
tensely under the rigid burden of her shame.

> MARTIN
> Ease yourself, Mademoiselle. It is not
> a new thing for us.

Claire's eyes well up, and tears streak her temples. But,
despite this, we can sense her relief. Martin removes the
object. Claire's closed eyes are filled with tears.

> MARTIN
> (gently)
> Why are you so unhappy? We both
> have the same needs. There is no
> cause to grieve over them.

CONTINUED

CONTINUED

He crosses to the cupboard, secures a cloth, dampens it in a pail of water on the floor, and returns to the bed. He goes about the business of washing her clean. He separates her dead legs and continues washing her in such a way that we know he spares her nothing. He moves quickly and gently. Then he covers her again.

CLOSE CLAIRE

Her lips clenched, she appears to have held her breath through it all.

CLOSE MARTIN

as he regards her:

> MARTIN
> We are as God made us.

CLOSE CLAIRE

Mortified, she turns her face to the wall. Then, after a moment . . .

> CLAIRE
> (faintly)
> Thank you.

Martin's hand appears in the edge of the FRAME. With the back of his hand, he rubs away the sweat and tears.

FULL SHOT THE ROOM

Martin crosses and places the cloth back on the cupboard.

> MARTIN
> I have to go now. I have work to do.
> There is a cowbell on the floor beside
> you. You can reach it. Wherever I
> am, I shall hear you—as I do Maman
> when she calls for me.

He crosses to the door and turns back to her with a crisp command.

> MARTIN
> Do not cry anymore. It is of no use.

CONTINUED

CONTINUED

He EXITS the room, leaving the door open behind him.

OVERHEAD SHOT   CLAIRE

She groans her feverish agony. Then, with slow and awful
deliberateness, she grips the edge of the coarse sheet and
draws it upward shakily to reveal her legs. Fearfully, she
moves the trunk of her body in such a way that we know
she is desperately trying to infuse some life into her limbs.
There is not the slightest response.

CLAIRE'S POV: HER LEGS

They lie dead still.

PHOTO EFFECT

The image slowly becomes misty to symbolize the tears in
her eyes.

                                                    DISSOLVE:

INT.   MARTIN'S ROOM   NIGHT

Through the broken slats of the closed shutters, the room is
shrouded in moonlight. Although a slight physical improve-
ment is noticeable in Claire's appearance, she is still being
tormented by a nightmarish dream and physical pain.
Slowly, she twists into a confused wakefulness.

                         CLAIRE
              Nanny-Anne . . .

As she stares sightlessly, Nanny-Anne materializes. She is
seated at the side of the bed and holds a letter in her hand
as she READS it:

                    NANNY-ANNE
              My dear child. Serrat burned to the
              ground last night. There is no secret
              about it. Your father left a letter to
              all whom his act might concern.
              Everything is in perfect order. The
              insurance has been canceled. Your
              father's personal possessions down
              to his signet ring have been labeled
                    (MORE)

                                                CONTINUED

CONTINUED

> NANNY-ANNE (CONT'D)
> "For His Majesty's Government."
> The coroner, I'm told, will bring in a
> verdict of unsound mind. But you
> and I know that he had the right to
> do what he did. The degradation and
> vulgarization of his home was intol-
> erable. Life can impose humiliations
> on us. But we don't have to submit
> to them. We do not have to live.
> They found his body among the
> ashes. He and his house were one. It
> was right and proper that they
> should go together.

Claire turns her head TOWARD CAMERA. Her eyes look downward at the floor next to her bed.

CLAIRE'S POV: WHAT SHE SEES

The clearly distinguishable figure of Martin lying full-length
on the floor.

> CLAIRE'S VOICE (OS)
> Robert . . .

With animal alertness, Martin's eyes open. He quickly raises
his head.

CLAIRE

She does not react to having seen Martin.

> CLAIRE
> Robert . . . oh, Robert . . . please
> help me.

She reacts to a twinge of pain, and through it, we can see
consciousness beginning to return. There is another, sharper
pain. Suddenly, she clenches her teeth against the half-
understood renewal of an inexorable physical pressure.
Finally, her mind clears, and she understands the pressure.
Realizing that she has no choice, she whispers weakly.

> CLAIRE
> Monsieur. Monsieur Thibaut.

CONTINUED

CONTINUED

Martin ENTERS the SHOT. He looks down on her, but Claire averts his gaze.

> CLAIRE
> I'm sorry—I can't help myself.

For a moment, his vacant eyes are puzzled. Then he understands. He smiles.

> MARTIN
> You see—you are getting better. You
> never called me before. Always, I
> had to guess.

He kneels across the bed and opens the shutters.

> MARTIN
> I did not always guess in time.

He laughs softly, and EXITS the SHOT.

Claire turns morbidly to the window, and looks out. CAMERA MOVES IN over the bed, and looks out the window.

OUTSIDE, the summer air vibrates with a ceaseless chatter of cicadas. HOLD on a bush near the window. The bush has not yet flowered.

PROCESS

IN FULL CAMERA VIEW, THE PLANT BLOSSOMS INTO FLOWER. THEN THE NIGHT DISAPPEARS AND THE EARLY MORNING SUN RISES. IT BURNS IN SLOWLY WITH THE BLAZING HEAT OF SUMMER.

EXT.   LONG SHOT   (ZOOMAR)   THE VALLEY   DAY

CAMERA looks out from the deserted village to the distant countryside and the now-familiar highway. CAMERA ZOOMS BACK to the washed-out bridge and gully in the nearer distance. Now, pointed toward the bridge, CAMERA LOWERS, and begins to DOLLY FORWARD inquisitively. When CAMERA reaches the gully, it peers over and down the precipitous edge.

We SEE the remains of Claire's shattered car, now half-covered by the wild growth. At first, everything is still and lifeless around the car. But—then there is a sound and

CONTINUED

CONTINUED

flicker of movement. It becomes evident that someone is there.

Curiously, CAMERA DOLLIES IN through the leaves and branches to the broken door. There, standing as well as he can in the confined area, is Martin. His attention is focused on the rearview mirror. He has been trying to remove it, and we can see that his patience is wearing thin. Finally, he snorts his exasperation, and rips the mirror, bracket and all, out of its moorings. This done, he shakes the screws out of the eyeholes and begins to climb out of the car.

EXT. THE GULLY DAY

Martin clambers through the branches and to the ground. He examines the mirror with delight, then holds it up and looks curiously at his face.

INSERT THE MIRROR

Mostly, we see Martin's sad, visionary eyes. His face is dirty with occasional bloody scratches from the bramble. In repose, now, Martin is not the frightening spectre that Claire saw when she awoke. He has, rather, a gentle plaintiveness.

WIDE ANGLE MARTIN

He lowers the mirror and stuffs it into his pocket. He begins to climb out of the gully.

EXT. THE DESERTED VILLAGE SQUARE DAY

CAMERA ANGLE is on the stone wall which protects the flank of the square from the abrupt descent into the ravine on the other side. After a moment, Martin's hands appear—first one, then the other—as he catapults himself into the SQUARE. PAN with him as he half-runs down the deserted street.

EXT. THE LAVOIR DAY

At one side of the street, about a hundred yards from Martin's house, is an old lavoir. Although crumbling badly, it is still able to contain the water in its basin.

CONTINUED

CONTINUED

Martin stops here. He puts his hands and arms in the water and swishes them. He rubs his wet hands over his face several times. He reaches into his pocket and pulls out the mirror. He looks at his face and seems to be satisfied. As he returns the mirror to his pocket, he happens to look down at his chest. He brushes his bare chest and the dust flies. Abruptly, he picks up a pail that is on the ground. He fills the pail full of water and upends it over his head. This done, he fills the pail again ands sets out down the street toward his house.

INT. MARTIN'S HOUSE DAY

ANGLE ACROSS CLAIRE ON THE BED

ON Martin as he ENTERS. Claire is on the threshold of waking. In the passage of time, her hair has grown back to perhaps a quarter its original shoulder length. The fever is gone and her health is improved. Although the physical damage to her face is still evident, the deep gashes are now scabs; the puffed lips are normal; the bruises have faded; the cuts are scratches.

Martin sets the pail down next to the bed. He opens the slatted shutters to let the sun in full.

> MARTIN
> Time to wake, Mademoiselle.

Claire doesn't look at him.

> CLAIRE
> Is it? For what? I sleep, I wake—I
> sleep, I wake! To what end?

Martin is at a loss for an answer. Instead, he crosses to the cupboard. With his back to Claire, she steals a secretive look at him as he carefully selects a few rags.

> MARTIN
> One must be careful of bedsores.
> Maman had them. I had a hard time
> making them heal.

His rags selected, he recrosses to the bed.

CONTINUED

CONTINUED

> CLAIRE
> What is that for?

> MARTIN
> I'm going to wash your back.

Claire holds the edge of the sheet tight under her chin.

> CLAIRE
> I told you: I want to be left alone!

> MARTIN
> It would do no good.

With quiet strength, he draws the sheet out of her clutching hands until she finally lets go. He tosses the sheet to the far side of the bed. He slides his arms under her body.

> CLAIRE
> What are you . . .

He flips her face down on the bed. He wets his rag in the water and wrings it out.

> MARTIN
> When I am finished, I will bring you
> some bread I have baked.

As he washes from her shoulders down:

> MARTIN (CONT'D)
> I am still able to use the handmill in
> the village bakery . . .
> (musing)
> Of course, you will soon find out I
> am a clumsy baker—Maman often
> scolded me.

> CLAIRE
> (frozen fearful, but in spite
> of herself)
> Was your mother like you?

> MARTIN
> Oh, no. She's a little woman. But
> very strong. We worked side by side
> in the fields until she had to rest.

CONTINUED

CONTINUED

As he moves downward to her legs . . .

> CLAIRE
> How long ago?

> MARTIN
> It must be several years. I've forgot-
> ten. One year is like another now.

He finishes, stands erect.

> MARTIN
> There.

He bends over Claire and flips her from facedown to faceup.
She closes her eyes against the new misery of knowing that
she does feel better, as he stares at his handiwork.

> CLAIRE
> (cold tolerance)
> May I have the sheet.

But he is strangely silent. She peers at him secretively.

CLAIRE'S POV: MARTIN

He is staring at Claire's legs.

> MARTIN
> Your legs are like my mother's. I
> used to rub them. She said it eased
> her. I shall rub yours.

He commences to massage them gently.

> MARTIN (CONT'D)
> One day they may regain their
> strength.

CLOSE   CLAIRE

Her fearful heart is pounding so that she cannot avoid the
tears that seep through her tightened lids.

PREVIOUS SHOT   MARTIN

Although he does not look at Claire's face, he has an unexpected perceptiveness.

CONTINUED

CONTINUED

> MARTIN
>
> You cry so often. Why? Do I hurt
> you? Or perhaps the water is too
> cold. I could heat it. But the cold is
> better for you. You *are* better. It was
> like that with my dog. She began to
> feel better and whimper just like
> you.

> CLAIRE
>
> Your dog was an animal!
> > (then)
> I'm not crying for pain.

> MARTIN
>
> For what then?

> CLAIRE
>
> To be free of this shameful helpless-
> ness. But you would not understand.
> You have only one measure of
> suffering.

There is a sudden stillness. Claire peers down at Martin.

CLAIRE'S POV: MARTIN

He sits stock still. Suddenly, he covers his eyes as though
trying to hide.

> MARTIN
>
> Every man has his own measure.

PREVIOUS SHOT

Fearing what may come next, Claire resorts to trivialities.
She puts her hands to her head.

> CLAIRE
>
> My hair—it grows so slowly.

Martin uncovers his eyes. He looks at her.

> MARTIN
>
> It will grow with your strength.

CONTINUED

CONTINUED

> CLAIRE
>
> It doesn't matter. Stupid of me to
> care.

> MARTIN
>
> It's a good thing to care—even about
> little things.

He gets the sheet and places it neatly back over her. He
tosses his rags in the pail and returns them to the cupboard.
He fills the metal cup with milk and returns to Claire. Raising her on his arm, he sits behind her. As he offers her the
milk, she starts to cough deliberately. Martin waits patiently
until she falls back in exhaustion.

> MARTIN
>
> It's a bad habit. You should try to
> break it.

Angrily, Claire dashes the cup out of his hand and over the
sheet. Martin stands up quickly and Claire falls backward.
He stares at her.

> CLAIRE
> (violently)
> Go ahead! Kill me! You *are* a mad-
> man! Kill me!

> MARTIN
> (with no resentment)
> You see how strong you are becom-
> ing?

He crosses to a chest in the corner and produces another
rough and dry but clean sheet. As he exchanges it for the
wet one:

> MARTIN
>
> We have an old lavoir and a spring
> that never runs dry. Our women
> used to beat their linen clean with
> stones. Even without soap, it is a
> way that serves well enough.

CONTINUED

CONTINUED

The last piece of furniture in the room is a tall armoire that stands next to the chest. The doors which were once gayly painted are now faded. Martin opens the door.

> MARTIN
> See? I even washed your dress. But the bloodstains had turned brown. I could not wash them out.

ANGLE THE OPEN ARMOIRE

Claire's dress hangs beside another woman's dress that is worn and rusty black.

CLOSE CLAIRE

She looks at the dresses.

MARTIN

to INCLUDE the armoire.

> MARTIN
> It is my mother's. Her workday frock. She was wearing it that last time when she called me to take her to the cemetery. I dressed her in her best.

He closes the door and stands for a moment as if in pious recollection.

CLAIRE

uses the moment to study Martin carefully.

CLAIRE'S POV: MARTIN

CAMERA PANS DOWN: First, the eyes that are fixed so often on some secret, tragic vision. Then, the chest—strong, tapering to a thin waist. Then, the legs, straight and lean. At the bottom, his dusty, well-formed feet on the earthen floor.

PREVIOUS

Martin comes out of his reverie. He crosses back to the bed and sits on the edge, facing Claire.

CONTINUED

CONTINUED

>   MARTIN
>   (tenderly)
>   Why are you so unhappy?

>   CLAIRE
>   Haven't I reason enough?

>   MARTIN
>   Everyone has reason enough.

>   CLAIRE
>   I'm diseased—half-paralyzed. It may
>   be forever. If so, I shall lie in this
>   wretched place and rot.

>   MARTIN
>   You are not rotting. You are getting
>   well.

>   CLAIRE
>   But I'm different. Even if I'm well,
>   I'm dead here. I don't belong here.

>   MARTIN
>   (blankly stubborn)
>   But you have no place to go.

>   CLAIRE
>   I tell you if I don't get away from
>   here, I'll go mad—even though I have
>   nowhere to go—even though I'm all
>   alone.

>   MARTIN
>   You have me. You have my house.

Claire is so taken aback by the enormity of this declaration
that she laughs outright. Martin flushes. His resentment is
that of an offended callow youth.

>   MARTIN
>   Besides, you are not alone. There is
>   a man—another man. You call on
>   him in your sleep.
>   (MORE)

                                    CONTINUED

CONTINUED

> MARTIN (CONT'D)
> (mimics the crisp English
> version of the name)
> Robert! Robert! You do not call on
> me by name. It is Monsieur this and
> Monsieur that. My name is Martin.

> CLAIRE
> (wearily)
> Robert is dead.

> MARTIN
> So is everyone—except the two of us.
> I did not ask you to come here to die.
> I did not know you wanted to die. I
> had to work hard to save you. It took
> all my strength.

> CLAIRE
> Should I be grateful?

> MARTIN
> Perhaps . . . a little.

> CLAIRE
> (scornfully)
> I'm not. I never shall be.

> MARTIN
> (utterly confused)
> What do you want of me?

> CLAIRE
> I've told you—over and over—let me
> go. Why do you keep me here?

> MARTIN
> (a pause)
> You are all I have.

Claire is stunned, speechless at this incredible, blinding
statement. Martin continues to look at her helplessly for a
long moment. Then he rises, goes to the door, and exits.

CLOSE   CLAIRE

CONTINUED

CONTINUED

Her sad and tortured eyes reflect the incredible possibilities
in her woman's mind.

>   CLAIRE
>   (a hoarse whisper)
>   Don't let me pity him. Please—don't
>   let me pity him.

>   FADE OUT.

FADE IN:

EXT. THE VILLAGE STREET NIGHT

It is twilight. Martin, approaching CAMERA, is carrying Claire
in his arms. The sheet is wrapped around her.

>   CLAIRE
>   (shouting and struggling)
>   Let me go! Let me go!

>   MARTIN
>   Don't be foolish. You don't hurt me,
>   you only hurt yourself.

Suddenly, the masonry of a crumbling structure SHATTERS,
LOUDLY falling to the ground. Claire screams in fright as
Martin evades it.

>   MARTIN
>   Don't worry. It is always happening.

Martin continues until he reaches the square.

EXT. THE SQUARE NIGHT

Near the stone wall, there is a wide-spreading plane tree.
Under it Martin has stretched out a mattress on a trestle
table. Ahead of it lies the valley, now etched in the quickly
sinking sun. The automobiles and normal life, soundless in
the distance, lend a feeling of isolation.

Martin places Claire gently upon the mattress. She clutches
the sheet angrily about her.

>   CONTINUED

CONTINUED

> MARTIN
> At daybreak, a cool breeze comes
> down from the hills. You will sleep
> better here.

He leaves her and perches himself on the low retaining wall.
Peacefully, with nothing more to say, he sits in benign
silence. Claire's hair is longer, the scars less visible. She
lifts herself a little and looks about.

Several goats are munching on the thick grass nearby, their
BELLS occasionally TINKLING. A CHICK runs into the SHOT,
CHIRPING, and is answered by a CLUCK of the HEN that follows.
OVER THIS, there is the SOUND of SOFTLY RUNNING WATER.

Claire turns to see what is behind her on the village street.

CLAIRE'S POV: THE STREET

The old, crumbling castle with its tower—and, at the foot of
the tower, the great stone lavoir built out of the wall—the
spring running softly into the basin.

BACK TO CLAIRE

As she turns to look out at the valley again, the darkness of
night is settling. With an effort, she yields to ask:

> CLAIRE
> Does no one ever come here?

Martin starts slightly, as though snatched out of a dream.

> MARTIN

Why should anyone come? The road is broken and dangerous. There is nothing here for anyone to seek.

> CLAIRE
> Only the two of us.

> MARTIN
> No one is seeking us.

> CLAIRE
> But people did live here once.

CONTINUED

CONTINUED

>   MARTIN
>   Yes. This was their home.
>
>   CLAIRE
>   What happened to them?
>
>   MARTIN
>   The young men went to war. Many
>   of them did not come back. A har-
>   vest failed. That was the end.
>   (pause)
>   The government took away the chil-
>   dren. Their parents went with them.
>   The old people held out the longest.
>
>   CLAIRE
>   What about your mother?
>
>   MARTIN
>   Maman would not go. She owned the
>   land and her house. She had a right
>   to wait for me to come home.
>
>   CLAIRE
>   Where had you been?
>
>   MARTIN
>   (looks vaguely into the
>   distance)
>   Out there.
>
>   CLAIRE
>   For how long?

Martin tries hard to recall. But he can't.

>   MARTIN
>   I have forgotten.
>
>   CLAIRE
>   Why did you come back?

His face darkens suspiciously.

>   MARTIN
>   This is my home.

CONTINUED

CONTINUED

>   CLAIRE
>   (baiting him)
>   Where you think no one will find
>   you.

She can see Martin's displeasure, but she goes on deliberately, dangerously.

>   CLAIRE
>   You *are* hiding, aren't you? Someone
>   is tracking you down. Why? What
>   have you done?

Martin slides down from the wall, crosses to Claire, and
looms over her. Claire falls back, satisfied that she has
provoked this crisis. She stares at him defiantly.

>   CLAIRE
>   One day he will catch up with you.
>   Or, is it they? They will trace you
>   here.

>   MARTIN
>   (vehemently)
>   No!

>   CLAIRE
>   You're not sure. You *are* afraid. You
>   know as well as I do that it isn't
>   possible to live this way—like a
>   castaway on a desert island.

As suddenly as it came, Martin's anger drains. Plaintively,

>   MARTIN
>   You do not understand. You are a
>   foreigner—you do not know my
>   people. They have forgotten me.
>   They have forgotten our village. It is
>   dead. I am dead, too.

>   CLAIRE
>   You mean you wish you were?

                                        CONTINUED

CONTINUED

                    MARTIN
                    (shrugs)
        Sometimes. But death is no escape.

                    CLAIRE
        You won't escape alive either . . .
        and, then, one day you will be
        caught.

                    MARTIN
                    (perplexed)
        Why do you hate me?

                    CLAIRE
        You know why. You kept me alive,
        but for your own reasons. I want to
        be free—anywhere away from this
        awful place and you. You won't let
        me go. Isn't that enough?

Abruptly, Martin turns away from her and leaves.

It is now NIGHT.

Weakened by her own passion, Claire falls back on the
mattress. Realizing that she is outside and alone for the
first time, she tries desperately to move. She twists and
turns with all her strength. She pulls and tugs at her dead
limbs trying to get into a sitting position. Ultimately, she
falls back in total exhaustion. And as she lies in the strange
stillness of this eerie place, her eyes reflect a growing
concern; they dart to strange little SOUNDS which occasionally
penetrate the stillness. Her body grows tense as her fear
increases. Now, from the old belfry church tower, an OWL
HOOTS. She turns to the SOUND, terrified. Overhead, a bird
frisks in the branches of the plane tree. On the ground
nearby, an animal skitters through the grass.

                    CLAIRE
                    (in a panic)
        Martin! Martin Thibaut!

She turns and looks in the direction he has gone.

CLAIRE'S POV:

                                        CONTINUED

CONTINUED

In the distant shadows of the street, there is a waving light.

CLAIRE

covers her mouth to avoid screaming in terror at the unknown gloomy sight.

CLAIRE'S POV:

Finally, Martin materializes in the darkness. He is carrying a lamp. In his other hand, he holds a dish.

WIDE ANGLE CLAIRE

Martin ENTERS the SHOT shyly, as though embarrassed by this ceremony. He hitches his lantern to the branch of a tree.

> MARTIN
> This is your first night in the open,
> Mademoiselle Claire. You see, I have
> killed and cooked a chicken for you.

He raises her and sits behind her so that she is forced to lean against his shoulder. She shudders as his arms encircle her, and he places the plate of food in her lap.

> MARTIN (CONT'D)
> Eat with your fingers, it will be
> easier.

Claire turns her face away.

> MARTIN (CONT'D)
> The meat next to the bone is the
> best.

> CLAIRE
> (sullenly)
> I'm not hungry.

> MARTIN
> (annoyed)
> Eat! I don't like to kill things. It
> seems to be God's will that we
> should—but to kill to no purpose is
> shameful.

CONTINUED

CONTINUED

                         CLAIRE
          Do you always kill with a purpose,
          Monsieur Martin?

                         MARTIN
                (with an edge of fury)
          Eat!

Claire feels the authority. Unwillingly, she obeys him. But
her need of food cannot be denied. And, once she starts, she
discovers that she is fiercely hungry. As he watches,
Martin's frown fades; he begins to smile with naïve pleasure
at Claire's lusty appetite.

INT. MARTIN'S ROOM   DAY   (EARLY MORNING)

Martin is massaging Claire's legs. He finishes, covers her.

                         MARTIN
          I was born in this bed.

He grows silent and looks at Claire with a new and tender
warmth.

                         CLAIRE
          Must you look at me that way?

                         MARTIN
                (almost to himself)
          Mademoiselle Claire . . .
                (awkwardly explaining)
          It is on your passport. A lovely
          name. In our language it means
          "light."

                         CLAIRE
          It was badly chosen for me.

                         MARTIN
          At first, it's true, you were dark. But
          now the light is coming through
          again.

She looks at him, surprised at his emergence from crude
simplicity.

                                        CONTINUED

CONTINUED

> MARTIN (CONT'D)
> It is because you are getting well.
> Look at your hands.

INSERT CLAIRE'S HANDS

They are placed on her chest. Relaxed.

> MARTIN'S VOICE
> They are becoming brown and strong
> like mine.

The hands suddenly clench.

PREVIOUS

> CLAIRE
> My hands were always strong!

> MARTIN
> (laughs, good-humored)
> There! You see—when a woman is
> angry like that, you don't have to
> worry about her.

> CLAIRE
> (bitterly)
> What do you know of women?!

His laughter dies quickly.

Like a rejected, disappointed child, Martin rises and EXITS
the room. Claire reaches out her hand after him, automatically regretful, almost on the brink of calling him back. She
thinks better of it and lets him go.

> FADE OUT.

FADE IN:

EXT. SKY DAY

Scudding clouds drift in front of the lowering sun. Suddenly
the sky is lashed by a bolt of lightning, then another. It
darkens as the SOUND of THUNDER roars.

EXT. DESERTED STREET (A SCHOOLHOUSE) DAY

> CONTINUED

CONTINUED

ANGLE on the schoolhouse and the blackness that lies beyond the open door. Abruptly, it begins to SHOWER. Presently, from the darkness of the schoolroom, Martin ENTERS hurriedly. He holds several ancient, dog-eared books as he looks up at the sky and the downpour of RAIN. He bolts forward, toward the square.

EXT. THE SQUARE DAY

Claire lies in her customary place near to but not now protected by the plane tree. The sudden shower is drenching her. But in the distance we can SEE Martin racing toward her. Reaching her, he drags the trestle bed under the protective covering of the tree.

CLAIRE AND MARTIN

Claire's hair is longer still; her healed face and body are starting to get brown.

> MARTIN
> (breathing hard)
> We needed it. But it is sad for you.

With the edge of Claire's sheet, he dries her face.

> MARTIN
> At this time of year, they come. It
> will be over soon.

Now he remembers the tattered books in his hand. He slaps them together and the dust rises.

> MARTIN (CONT'D)
> I found them in the old schoolroom.

He holds the books out to Claire.

> MARTIN (CONT'D)
> Perhaps they will help to pass the
> time. They're good stories.

> CLAIRE
> (murmurs)
> Thank you.

CONTINUED

CONTINUED

He looks for some sign of her pleasure. Not knowing what else to say or do, he slaps the books together again several times to clean them. The dust is so heavy, it makes him cough. When he stops, he looks at Claire proudly.

> MARTIN
> . . . but you don't cough anymore.
> Only when you remember.

Now the shower has stopped as abruptly as it started. The sun is sinking, but it is warm.

> MARTIN (CONT'D)
> You see? It is all over.

He pulls the bed back into the sun. Meanwhile:

> MARTIN (CONT'D)
> Soon you will be dry again.

Now, obviously discomfited by her trenchant silence, he crosses to the wall and sits, like a faithful dog, facing her. Presently, in an almost involuntary sense of pity,

> CLAIRE
> You must be very lonely.

Her comment seems to have found a mark. He rises and crosses to her. He stands mute, looking into her face. Claire feels her fear returning.

> CLAIRE
> Why are you staring at me?

> MARTIN
> Your hair. In the shade it's raven
> black. In the sunlight, there is gold in
> it. It's beautiful again.

> CLAIRE
> (coldly, almost roughly)
> What do you know of beauty?

> MARTIN
> I lived once with a city woman—like
> you. She had lovely things about her.
> (MORE)

CONTINUED

CONTINUED

> MARTIN (CONT'D)
>
> At first I was afraid of them. But she taught me—a little—to see them as she did.

> CLAIRE
>
> Did you love her?

> MARTIN
>
> Yes.

> CLAIRE
>
> What happened to her?

> MARTIN
>
> She died.

> CLAIRE
> (at a loss)
>
> You're not lucky in your women, Monsieur Martin—one dead, one dying.

> MARTIN
>
> You are not dying.

> CLAIRE
>
> I shall die. One can will oneself to die.

> MARTIN
>
> Don't! Don't! Why should you?

> CLAIRE
>
> Why shouldn't I? What is there for me to live for? You have been kind—after your fashion. You say I have your home and you. I'm sorry—it's not enough. It never could be.

His characteristic and sudden childish petulance rises in him. He reaches in his pocket and takes out a sheet of paper and pencil. He tosses them to her.

CONTINUED

CONTINUED

> MARTIN
> Very well. Write to this man—this
> Robert. Send for him.

Claire feels her blood mounting with this new challenge.

> CLAIRE
> I told you—he's dead.

> MARTIN
> You were not calling on a dead man.

> CLAIRE
> People can be alive and dead to each
> other.

> MARTIN
> People quarrel. But they come to-
> gether again. They make peace. Ask
> him to come here for you. I will see
> that the letter goes to Draguignan. In
> a few days your Robert could be
> here.

Claire watches him narrowly with deepening distrust.

> CLAIRE
> If he came—if people came here—
> what would it mean to you?

> MARTIN
> (quivers at the thought)
> It would be as you said—I should be
> caught.

> CLAIRE
> Why? For what?

> MARTIN
> What the man in the black robe said
> . . . long ago . . . that I am danger-
> ous.

> CLAIRE
> Were you? Are you?

CONTINUED

CONTINUED

Martin covers his face to hide.

> MARTIN
> I don't know—I don't know.

Claire lets the pencil fall to the ground. She crumples the piece of paper and tosses it away.

> CLAIRE
> Don't be afraid. I shan't write. I
> think you knew I wouldn't.

With a great effort, Martin regains his calm.

> MARTIN
> The sun will be down soon. It will be
> damp out here tonight. I must carry
> you in.

With the books in his hand, he lifts her. Claire holds herself stiff with hostility as he starts for his house.

> MARTIN
> (sadly)
> Why do you pull away from me?

> CLAIRE
> You're dirty and sweaty and half-
> naked. You disgust me!

> MARTIN
> (the angry boy)
> But I'm not dirty. I work in the
> fields. It's hot work. I should be a
> fool to wear the clothes of city folk.
> In the winter, I wear a shirt and
> coat—you'll see.

> CLAIRE
> Please God—no. I shall be gone.

> MARTIN
> Where?

Claire begins to sob in desperation.

CONTINUED

CONTINUED

> MARTIN (CONT'D)
> There! You are crying again. You
> are like me. When we are hurt, we
> both cry like children.

CAMERA HOLDS, as Martin continues on with Claire toward the house.

INT. MARTIN'S ROOM DAY

The shutters are closed, and it is moderately dark. Martin ENTERS with Claire and lays her on the bed. He smoothes the sheet over her, and places the books at her side. He crosses to the armoire, where he searches inside and finds a candle stump. He shows it to Claire.

> MARTIN
> If you want to read later, this will
> give you light enough.

He takes a match from his pocket and lights the candle. On a board near Claire's bed, he melts a small pool of wax and sets the stub in it.

> MARTIN
> I may be gone all night. A young
> nanny goat is having her first kid.
> She may need me, too. Don't be
> afraid to be alone.

> CLAIRE
> (lying)
> I'm not afraid of loneliness. Aren't
> you afraid that someone will see the
> light?

> MARTIN
> The road is too far off. No one
> comes.
> (points to the candle)
> Be careful to blow it out before you
> sleep.

He places the COWBELL near her.

CONTINUED

CONTINUED

> MARTIN (CONT'D)
> Ring if you need help. I shall hear
> you and come at once.

> CLAIRE
> I shan't ring.

> MARTIN
> It might be more comfortable for
> you, and easier for me.

He crosses to the door and hesitates. He savors the hope
that she will say something—he struggles with some final
appeal of his own. But words are beyond his reach.

> MARTIN
> (finally)
> Good night, Mademoiselle Claire.

Claire does not answer. Martin EXITS.

At first Claire lies perfectly still. Then she raises her hands
in front of her face. She clenches her fists tightly, then tests
the power of one hand against the other. She squeezes them
together, recognizing their unusual strength.

She feels her arms—lean and hard. She presses her hands
against her stomach—it is flat and strong. She places her
hands over and around her breasts. She smiles ironically at
their well-rounded firmness.

Now, as if to make the supreme test, she takes a deep
breath and exhales. Her lungs are clear and untrammeled. A
little laugh escapes her.

> CLAIRE
> (sardonically)
> Rest, sunshine, and good plain food.

She leans out of her bed and picks up the board with its
fluttering candle. She blows out the light. The room goes to
complete darkness.

INT. A DECAYED, DISINTEGRATED BARN NIGHT

The area is lighted by the lantern Martin was earlier carrying. In dead stillness, he attends the mother goat until, as

CONTINUED

CONTINUED

though suddenly alerted by some eerie presence, he stops what he is doing and stares intently ahead.

CLOSE MARTIN

His eyes express some serious concern. Apparently, something is becoming fixed in his mind. He rises and EXITS the barn quickly.

EXT. THE DESERTED STREET NIGHT

Martin runs toward his house, his lantern lighting the way.

INT. MARTIN'S ROOM NIGHT

ANGLE ACROSS CLAIRE to the door.

Claire is writhing in the toils of some agony. Her eyes closed, her hands and teeth clenched, she groans as Martin appears in the doorway, his lantern lighting the room. He goes to the bed and raises the lantern close over Claire's head. Claire half-opens her fevered, frowning eyes.

> MARTIN
> What is it, Mademoiselle Claire?

> CLAIRE
> (defiantly)
> Nothing . . . nothing . . .

> MARTIN
> You are in pain.

> CLAIRE
> How did you know?

> MARTIN
> I felt it.

As the ceaseless torment continues, Claire rolls her head from side to side feverishly.

> CLAIRE
> It's an earache. Haven't had one
> since I was a child.

> MARTIN
> I had it once—it's a bad thing. I will
> be back.

CONTINUED

CONTINUED

As he goes—

> CLAIRE
> (in agony)
> Ohhh . . . Nanny-Anne . . . it hurts
> so . . .

Martin returns and kneels anxiously at Claire's side. He rests his hand on the bed; it is bloodstained and befouled. Claire takes his hand and clings to it. Martin is moved by this.

> MARTIN
> I am heating a poultice—you can hold
> it close to the pain. Maman used to
> make it.

Half hearing, Claire groans and drives her nails into Martin's flesh.

> MARTIN
> Why don't you cry? You cry over
> other foolish things.

> CLAIRE
> (a twisted smile)
> But not from pain. None of us ever
> cries from pain. It just isn't done.

> MARTIN
> I don't cry from pain either.

> CLAIRE
> From what, then?

> MARTIN
> From being alone. Even with Maman
> waiting for me, I am sometimes
> lonely. When I tell her, she says:
> "Everyone is alone, my son. Wait."

Releasing his hand, he EXITS. Claire cannot avoid looking after him—reacting tragically to his madness. Soon he returns with the poultice. He resumes the position on his knees and tentatively applies the hot rag to her ear.

CONTINUED

CONTINUED

> MARTIN
>
> Is it too hot?

> CLAIRE
>
> It's good.

She rests her ear against it, facing Martin.

> CLAIRE (CONT'D)
>
> Thank you.

> MARTIN
>
> Does it feel better?

> CLAIRE
>
> I think—a little.

> MARTIN
>
> Have patience. Sooner or later,
> everything passes.

He sits on the floor and gives her his hand. She takes it and looks at the blood.

> CLAIRE
>
> How is your goat?

> MARTIN
>
> Very proud. Her kid is a fine young
> fellow.

> CLAIRE
>
> (smiles warmly)
> Do you know the worst pain in the
> world, Martin?

> MARTIN
>
> (with boyish interest)
> No. What is it?

> CLAIRE
>
> Dr. John told me. He said, "It's the
> pain you've got." He made me
> laugh.

They laugh together.

CONTINUED

CONTINUED

> MARTIN
> Well, that's true.

Claire looks at him sadly for a long moment. In his embarrassment, Martin awkwardly tries to fill the gap.

> MARTIN
> I'm not much to look at, Mademoiselle Claire—a rough fellow. But not
> dirty. I used to shave—but when you
> have no soap and only a blunt
> razor—it hurts. Besides, my goats
> don't care—they wear beards, too.

Claire laughs. He rubs his cheek ruefully.

> MARTIN (CONT'D)
> Now that you're here, I'll try again.

But by now Claire has closed her eyes in peaceful exhaustion. Martin sits, scarcely breathing, worshiping her slumber.

> FADE OUT.

FADE IN:

INT. MARTIN'S ROOM DAY

The sun is slanting through the shutter. Claire opens her eyes as though recovering from an ugly dream. She turns her head to discover Martin, asleep. His head lies on the edge of the bed as he sits, half-crouched, on the floor. Now Claire's gaze is held fast by something.

CLAIRE'S POV:

Claire's hand is clasped in Martin's.

CLAIRE

Her lips tighten, anguished at the pitiful sight. She withdraws her hand, and, as she does, she looks down at the floor.

CLAIRE'S POV: KNIFE

CONTINUED

CONTINUED

The knife that Martin hastily placed there the night before when he came from the stable.

WIDE ANGLE

Stealthily, Claire reaches for the knife and gets it just as Martin stirs and awakens. She quickly secretes the knife at her side. Martin smiles at her.

> MARTIN
> You are better. It is in your face.

Unnerved lest Martin should find the knife, Claire's antagonism returns. Martin notices but pretends not to.

> MARTIN (CONT'D)
> I will be able to go to the valley
> today. I now have produce enough to
> exchange for the things we need.

He waits a moment, hoping she will say something. But she is silent. He stands up.

> MARTIN (CONT'D)
> It's a day's march from here, but
> don't be afraid—Maman will keep
> watch over you. If you call her, she
> will comfort you.

Claire is suddenly swept by a surge of uncontrollable fury.

> CLAIRE
> Your mother's dead! Don't you
> understand? She's dead! And you're
> mad! Really mad!

Martin is stunned at this sudden onslaught.

> CLAIRE (CONT'D)
> Go on—I'm not afraid of you any-
> more. I detest you for what you are
> and what you're doing to me! And
> now I'm on the verge of madness
> myself. But I won't let you do it to
> me! I won't go mad! I won't!

CONTINUED

CONTINUED

Swiftly, she raises the knife to plunge it into her breast. But, as though instinctively forewarned, he snatches the blade from her hand and, almost simultaneously, he slaps her a stinging blow across the cheek. For a long moment, they stare at each other over the gulf of their profound differences—a gulf that has suddenly become narrower. Claire rubs her cheek.

> CLAIRE
> That was rough, Monsieur Martin.

> MARTIN
> I am sorry. I did not mean to hurt
> you. It does not matter what you do
> to me—but to take your life is an
> offense against God.

He throws the knife into a corner. Then he bends over and lifts her with her sheet. With Claire in his arms, he EXITS the room.

FADE OUT:

FADE IN:

EXT. THE SQUARE DAY

It is late afternoon; the sun is setting. Claire is lying on a broad sheet that Martin has placed on the grass under a large, lush plane tree. Behind her back, a large straw pillow helps her to sit almost erect. Set out within easy reach are little mounds of food: wild strawberries, blackberries, and grapes, each set on its own cabbage leaf: bread, milk, and cheese. Close by, ambling on its tottering legs, is the newborn kid, tied by a cord anchored next to Claire's hand. From behind the tree, the mother watches with horn-tossing pride. A few chickens scratch about.

Claire sets down the book she has been reading. For the first time, she is herself—her guard completely down. She pulls the kid toward her. Soaking some bread in milk, she feeds him, and he nuzzles her hand as he eats it.

CONTINUED

CONTINUED

> CLAIRE
> You sweet, sweet darling . . .
> (then)
> I almost forgot—you do love cheese,
> don't you. Of course your own
> mother's cheese.

And, the kid proves that he does. There is the SOUND of a
SNORT, and Claire looks toward it.

CLAIRE'S POV: THE MOTHER GOAT

has ventured forward, threatening.

BACK TO SCENE

> CLAIRE
> Now, mother, let's not be jealous.

The goat shakes her head up and down. Claire laughs and
holds out some bread. The goat comes forward and takes her
offering. She quickly becomes inquisitive about the other
food. Claire playfully pushes her away.

> CLAIRE
> Oh, no you don't. That's mine.

Claire commences to grab the food and eat hungrily, laugh-
ing and warding off the insistent, comic goat.

> CLAIRE (CONT'D)
> All right, stop pushing.
> (she concedes to the goat)
> I'm sure there must be a can you'd
> enjoy more.

A PAIR OF LEGS, the feet covered by espadrilles, ENTER the
FRAME. Claire glimpses the legs from the corner of her eye
and is startled. She looks up.

TWO SHOT CLAIRE AND MARTIN

He is smiling pleasantly. He holds a book in his hand.

CONTINUED

CONTINUED

> CLAIRE
> Will you please make some sounds so
> that I know when you're here?

Martin squats to the ground and hands her the book.

> CLAIRE
> What's this? A Bible?

> MARTIN
> The collabo is a Protestant. He
> doesn't believe in anything. He gave
> it to me against a batch of eggs.

Claire scans the brown-edged pages of the old book.

> CLAIRE
> Even in French, the phrases are still
> familiar.

> MARTIN
> Did you once go to church?

> CLAIRE
> (nods)
> It seems so long ago.

> MARTIN
> You have told me about your
> school—where you learned French—
> but you have not told me about your
> church.

> CLAIRE
> It was a lovely chapel where all the
> well-bred young ladies had trouble
> keeping awake.
> (the memory is too much;
> she gives up)
> But it's all gone now. One night my
> father burned our house down and
> died with it. People said he was mad.

> MARTIN
> But he wasn't. He was like the great
> lord who once lived in our castle.
> (MORE)

CONTINUED

CONTINUED

>   MARTIN (CONT'D)
> When the besiegers came and he
> knew they were too strong, he blew
> himself up. Our peasants killed their
> women so they would not be out-
> raged.

>   CLAIRE
>   (sadly)
> Are we all alike, Martin? Do we all
> suffer for what we love? In the end,
> are we all defeated?

>   MARTIN
> This man—this lover of yours—this
> Robert. What about him?

>   CLAIRE
> He was wonderful. He had a genius
> for living. He was like life itself.

>   MARTIN
>   (hotly)
> He was worthless. You didn't even
> love him. Love isn't like that.

>   CLAIRE
> What is love to you?

>   MARTIN
>   (austerely)
> Our people don't talk much of love.
> But we are faithful.

>   CLAIRE
> Are you?

>   MARTIN
> We make a contract. It is not for love
> or happiness. It is for life. Sometimes
> some of us break our contracts. That
> is our foolishness and to our shame.
> This man and you had no contract.
> You were both lawless and without
> roots. When the summer heat came,
>   (MORE)

CONTINUED

CONTINUED

> MARTIN (CONT'D)
> and the drought, you knew that what
> he was to you would wither and die.
> So, in time, you ran away from him.

> CLAIRE
> (surprised at his
> shrewdness)
> That's not true. How could you
> understand? Robert would have
> stood by me. It was I who loved him
> too much to let him spoil his life.

Martin looks at her in contemptuous silence. His silence silences Claire.

> MARTIN
> (finally)
> I'd better take you in now.

He lifts her and starts carrying her to the house.

EXT. THE DESERTED STREET DAY

Martin is pushing something in front of him; it makes quite a clatter on the cobblestones. It is a handmade contraption consisting of an old armchair with two large wooden wheels attached to the sides. A blanket lies on the chair.

His eyes are bright with triumph as he stops in front of the house. He removes the blanket and drops it on the ground. He enters the house and soon reappears with Claire in his arms, wrapped in her sheet. She is annoyed but curious.

> MARTIN
> You see? Now you will be able to
> wheel yourself outdoors. If the
> wheels hurt your hands, you can
> cover them with rags—like gloves.
> You are strong enough.

He places her in the chair and picks up the blanket. He unfolds it and reveals a sort of serape which he has made by cutting a hole in the center. He places it over her head and removes the sheet.

CONTINUED

CONTINUED

> MARTIN (CONT'D)
> Now try it.

Claire is exhilarated and eagerly venturesome. With the wild elation of a caged animal suddenly and wonderfully re-leased, she seizes the wheels and pushes the chair forward. It spins out of control and falls ludicrously against the wall.

> CLAIRE
> (almost as if to shock
> Martin)
> Sale vache!

Then she laughs as Martin straightens the chair and gets her started.

> CLAIRE
> All right—I've got it. Let's go.

She takes over, vigorously pushing the wheels forward on the uneven cobbles along the street with Martin, close by, sometimes straightening her erratic course, sometimes lending his strength—their happy laughter is joined.

EXT. THE SCHOOLHOUSE DAY

They ENTER the SHOT. Claire stops then moves her chair close to one of the blank, sightless windows and peers into the schoolroom.

> MARTIN
> This was our schoolroom.

INT. THE SCHOOLROOM (CLAIRE'S POV) DAY

All that remains are the old, rotted pine desks. A teacher's pulpit is in front; behind it is a blackboard. Chalked on the blackboard in a child's hand is the equation: $5 + 6 = 11$.

EXT. THE SCHOOLHOUSE DAY

Martin leaves Claire and enters the room. As he goes,

> MARTIN
> I will show you something.

Claire peers into the window.

CLAIRE'S POV: THE SCHOOLROOM

INT. THE SCHOOLHOUSE DAY

Martin approaches a desk and runs his hand over the lid,
raising a cloud of dust. His VOICE when he talks is like a
DISEMBODIED SOUND.

> MARTIN
> It was mine. Our teacher made me
> sit in front because I was such a bad,
> stupid little boy. But when he wasn't
> looking, I carved my name.

He laughs aloud, and it sounds ghostly.

EXT. THE SCHOOLHOUSE DAY

Claire forlornly pulls herself away from the window. Again,
the chair turns wildly, almost spilling her. Martin appears
in time to see the result and hear her.

> CLAIRE
> Damn you!

He laughs, helps her right the chair, and sets it in motion
again.

EXT. THE STREET (MOVING SHOT) DAY

Claire looks into the gaping doorways of the crumbling ruins
of buildings whose dark interiors show the squalid dissolu-
tion of broken chairs, mildewed mattresses, shattered glass,
and other debris.

> CLAIRE
> I'd like to see the inside of your
> castle.

> MARTIN
> It would not be safe. But I will show
> you our church, and you will see if it
> is like your chapel.

He guides the chair forward.

EXT. THE CHURCH DAY

Martin, without stopping, pushes the chair into the church.

INT. THE CHURCH DAY

CONTINUED

CONTINUED

Martin wheels the chair into the center of the scene. It is the same as it was when we first saw it, except that the sunlight streaming through the broken windows brings the colors of the frescoes more vividly alive. Claire stares at them in astonishment.

CLAIRE'S POV: THE FRESCOES

> CLAIRE'S VOICE
> They're beautiful.

> MARTIN'S VOICE
> You see, I am not so poor. Once I asked Monsieur Le Cure to explain them to me. He just said, "They're very old, Martin." Sometimes just to be old is important.

Martin ENTERS the SHOT

He points to the bright-hued little demon gleefully forking some wailing sinner into the red maw of hell.

> MARTIN
> I always like this little fellow—much better than the saints. I told Maman, and she explained that perhaps he wasn't really a devil but a boy like myself who hadn't been properly brought up.

WIDE ANGLE

Martin crosses to the altar, gets a rag, and returns to the fresco. As he goes and comes,

> MARTIN (CONT'D)
> She said I was lucky that I had been taught to be kind and courteous. Even to people I didn't like. She said that cruelty is the one great sin.

Now, with the rag, he carefully wipes the dust off the frescoes.

CONTINUED

CONTINUED

CLOSE   CLAIRE

Tears well in her eyes. As she watches him, the sun disappears and Claire raises her eyes to the gloom.

> CLAIRE
> Don't come for him—whoever you
> are. He's quite harmless. I'll vouch
> for that.

Just then, a breeze stirs her hair, and a BELL overhead
SOUNDS lightly. Claire looks up toward the sound.

FULL SHOT   THE CHURCH

> MARTIN
> Maman is calling us.

Claire's expression remains benign. For the first time, his
hallucination no longer troubles her. Martin starts moving
the chair out.

EXT.   CEMETERY ENTRANCE   DAY

Martin pushes the wheelchair along the rough track leading
to the gate and into the cemetery. As he leads her through
the teetering crosses and tin wreathes,

CLAIRE'S POV: WHAT SHE SEES

The porcelain portrait of a girl in her best dress. Under it,
the legend: MON AMOUR. PAN TO: a soldier in uniform. The
legend: MORT POUR LA PATRIE. PAN TO a gray-haired, fierce-
eyed old man. The legend: NOTRE GRANDPÉRE CHÉRI.

And now we HOLD at the grave of Martin's mother; he
pushes the chair up to the very edge. The rosebushes have
now lost their petals. Martin kneels and pats the grave
gently.

> MARTIN
> Maman, I have brought Mademoiselle
> Claire to visit you as I promised. She
> is much stronger now—almost well—
> except that she can't walk. I mended
> your old wheelchair for her. She
> wants to meet you, too.

CONTINUED

CONTINUED

He looks at Claire. Uncomfortably, she smoothes her hair and draws the serape closer—almost as if she wants to make a good impression.

> MARTIN
> She is a quiet woman. She never
> talks much—even to me. But she's
> glad you've come.

Claire seems unable to speak.

> MARTIN (CONT'D)
> She is good and kind. When I came
> home, she was waiting. She took care
> of me—and hid me. There was no
> other woman like her.

> CLAIRE
> But there *was* another woman.

> MARTIN
> (his eyes cloud)
> She was different. She was like you.

He rises and is about to leave.

> CLAIRE
> Martin . . .

He stops.

> CLAIRE (CONT'D)
> When I am dead, bury me here.
> Don't put up any cross—no one need
> ever know.

> MARTIN
> Maman says you are not going to
> die.

> CLAIRE
> Did she tell you what is to become of
> me?

> MARTIN
> She says God knows.

CONTINUED

CONTINUED

> CLAIRE
>
> But I told you; I don't believe in him.

> MARTIN
>
> He doesn't mind. He will still take
> care of you.

He looks at the grave worshipfully. Seeing this, Claire lays her hand on the grave's foot.

> CLAIRE
>
> Goodbye, Madame.

> MARTIN
>
> (murmurs)
> Thank you.

He turns the chair and starts to push it out of the cemetery.

EXT. THE SQUARE NIGHT

The moon shines through the leaves of the plane tree where Claire lies in her makeshift bed, unable to sleep. She glances surreptitiously across the ground to where Martin lies bedded down in his customary place on the grass.

CLAIRE'S POV: MARTIN

He turns a few times. Then, lifting himself on his elbow, he looks toward Claire.

MARTIN'S POV: CLAIRE

She lies perfectly still, knowing that Martin is looking.

BACK TO SCENE

Martin gets up quietly. He begins to pace, as if in the throes of some desperate desire. Finally, he approaches Claire. He looks down at her face. SIMULT, with amazing suddenness, a gust of violent wind blows across the square, sending the leaves flying. Martin raises his hand as if to lay it upon Claire. Almost at the same moment, the BELL TOLLS in the TOWER. Martin snatches his hand back. He stands a moment longer, thinking, then walks off into the shadows of the street.

CONTINUED

CONTINUED

CLOSE CLAIRE

She opens her eyes cautiously to see that he has gone. Now, tormented, she looks up into the branches of the tree.

> CLAIRE
> Oh, God help me—let me escape.

The wind grows fiercer, flailing the branches in its fury, shooting the leaves across Claire, hair flying, sheet rippling. Birds fly by, loudly flapping their wings, and animals begin to dart. Then, as if answering her plea, the BELL begins to TOLL LOUDER, FRANTICALLY.

Finally:

> CLAIRE
> Stop it! Stop it!

But the BELL CONTINUES.

> CLAIRE
> I've done nothing to your son. I owe
> him nothing! I pity him, but he's
> nothing to me!

The BELL RINGS MORE FRANTICALLY.

> CLAIRE
> Stop it! Please! Stop it . . . I beg
> you . . .

Abruptly, there is a horrifying crash as the huge bell falls to the ground. The SOUND of TEARING METAL AND CRUMBLING MASONRY is followed by a vast silence.

Panic-stricken, Claire struggles to pull herself up. And heedless of the meaning it has for her, her body responds as she shifts her legs off the bed so that she sits with them dangling over the edge. But the moment passes, and in the next instant all her awareness centers on the realization of what she has just done. Slowly, an expression comes into her face that is stronger than terror: the flashing comprehension that she has just moved freely.

Claire looks down at her legs. Cautiously, incredulously, as the wind howls about her, she tries them again. First, she

CONTINUED

CONTINUED

raises one tremulous leg up and down again. Next, the other responds as well. Finally, she stretches them both out and down again.

Silently, now, she begins to cry and, weakened by the miracle, she falls back upon the bed and looks up through her grateful tears into the black, windswept branches of the tree.

> CLAIRE
> There is a god. He's heard my
> prayers.

At the same moment, as though this is the final answer, rain begins to fall heavily. The rain splashes through the foliage onto her upturned face. The wind abates.

> MARTIN'S VOICE (OS)
> Mademoiselle Claire . . . Mademoi-
> selle Claire . . .

Martin ENTERS, holding his lantern. He is distraught.

> MARTIN
> (shouting)
> The bell! The devil has torn down
> her bell! She will never call me
> again! I shall never hear her . . .
> never . . . never . . .

Claire looks at him piteously.

> CLAIRE
> Perhaps you can hang it up again.

> MARTIN
> No—no, it's broken. He cut its rope,
> and it crashed through the church
> roof. It lies in pieces before the altar.

He gathers himself long enough to look at Claire and see that the rain is soaking her.

> CLAIRE
> You'd better take me inside, Martin.

CONTINUED

CONTINUED

He grows quiet and resigned. As he lifts her in his arms, Claire gives no sign, no involuntary movement that might betray her condition. And, as the storm continues, Martin walks with Claire, disappearing into the black, deserted street.

INT. MARTIN'S ROOM DAY

It is early morning. Claire lies rigidly on the bed, pretending to be asleep. Martin sits on the floor, his arms about his knees, his brilliant gaze fixed upon Claire. Although tranquil, his look reveals that something has left him puzzled. Meanwhile, Claire looks at him through veiled eyes, wondering. Finally, she can stand the duel no longer. She opens her eyes to him, but he continues to stare at her silently.

> CLAIRE
> Have you been sitting up like that all
> night?

> MARTIN
> (strangely suspicious)
> Yes. I don't know. I'm afraid. I think
> something's happened.

Claire closes her eyes to shut out the unpredictable as Martin stands up, comes to the window, and pushes the shutters open. The sun brightens the room. He looks darkly into Claire's face, then turns and EXITS the room.

Claire waits with baited breath, listening to the SOUND of his DEPARTING FOOTFALLS. Then, adjusting the sheet, she slips her legs over the bedside and sits up. With an effort, she raises herself to her feet. Her legs shake a little but hold her. She teeters cautiously to the door and makes it just before her legs give out. There, clinging to the lintel for support, she opens the door and looks out.

EXT. THE STREET (CLAIRE'S POV) DAY

A pale sunshine polishes the rain-cleansed cobbles. In the distance, she can see Martin standing by the great stone lavoir. He has removed his denim trousers, and, with an iron basin, he is pouring sunlit water over his naked body. Even at this distance, we can see that he is endowed with splendid life.

INT. THE ROOM DAY

Claire stands motionless, looking at Martin, apparently held by what she sees. But, as if to blot out her thoughts, she closes the door abruptly. Then, while glancing back at the door, she lurches over to the armoire and opens it.

ANGLE THE ARMOIRE

On one of the shelves, she finds her underclothes, rough-dried but neatly folded. With warm affection, she examines their condition, then, neatly folding them as they were, she replaces them on the shelf. Looking further, she finds her passport. She opens it.

INSERT: STANDARD PASSPORT WITH LARGE LETTERS: PERMIS DE SÉJOUR

BACK TO SCENE

She closes the passport and replaces it. She finds her hand-bag, searches it, and finds her wallet. She opens it and withdraws a bundle of francs. The money pleases her. She replaces the money, puts the wallet in the handbag, and returns it to its exact position.

Now she looks at the two dresses and removes her own. While she is inspecting the bloodstains, she hears Martin approaching. She quickly replaces the dress, closes the armoire door, and limps noiselessly back to her bed. She positions herself innocently just as Martin ENTERS the room.

In one hand, Martin holds a pail of water and some rags. In the other, and along his arm, he has a bowl of milk, a hunk of bread, and a square of cheese. He leans toward Claire and she takes the food.

> CLAIRE
> Thank you.

As Claire starts to eat hungrily, Martin sets the pail and rags on the floor. He secures a makeshift broom, and, busying himself like a careful woman, he sweeps out the dust and leaves that were blown into the room. He gives no sign of the previous night's agony, as if in his strange, intermittent madness, he has forgotten it.

CONTINUED

CONTINUED

>   MARTIN
> It will be hot today, Mademoiselle
> Claire. It is always so after a bad
> storm. It would be better for you to
> stay here till sundown.

By now, Claire has drunk her milk and eaten most of her
food. Martin takes the bowl and places it to one side on the
floor. Then he reaches for the sheet to strip Claire. But
Claire clings to it.

>   CLAIRE
> For the love of God, leave me alone!
> I'm not so helpless anymore!

Martin is taken aback. Claire quickly recognizes that she
may have exposed her new feelings.

>   CLAIRE
>   (quickly resigned)
> Oh, all right. Do as you please, it
> doesn't matter to me.

She turns her face away from Martin. But, this time, as
Martin goes about the ministrations of washing her, we can
SEE Claire set her teeth against some incalculable response
when he separates her legs.

>   MARTIN
>   (without looking)
> I thought you would be used to it by
> now.

>   CLAIRE
> I am. You are someone who is kind
> to me.

>   MARTIN
> It may be that I have done you
> wrong. You wanted so much to die.
>   (shrewdly)
> Do you still want to die?

Claire turns to look at him defiantly.

                                        CONTINUED

CONTINUED

>   CLAIRE
> No!

>   MARTIN
>   (darkly)
> Death can seem to be the only an-
> swer. But it is a terrible answer. A
> man can only make it once. If one
> waits—if one has patience—there
> may be another answer.

>   CLAIRE
>   (beguilingly)
> I haven't found it. I haven't even
> found myself. I don't know what I've
> become—not even what I look like. I
> must be hideous.

Martin stops his ministrations and looks at her.

>   CLAIRE
> Have the scars really healed?

He draws the sheet carefully over her. He crosses to the
small chest, opens a drawer, and removes the rearview
mirror that he took from Claire's car. He returns and hands
it to Claire. She takes it and lies still for a moment, wondering. She closes her eyes in order to conjure up the last
vision of herself in a mirror.

>   DISSOLVE TO:

MIRROR SHOT

It is the picture of Claire when she looked at herself last in
the mirror at Dr. Fenwick's office. But, to our surprise, we
are not in Dr. Fenwick's office.

INT.   A BACKSTAGE DRESSING ROOM   NIGHT

The dressing room is large and properly appointed as it
would be for a star. Claire is alone and seated at the dressing table. Dressed fashionably in street clothes, she is idly
smoking and checking her makeup in the mirror. After a
decent pause, there is a KNOCK on the DOOR. Claire opens it to
find:

>   CONTINUED

CONTINUED

                              CANDY
        Surprise!

                              CLAIRE
                            (gleefully)
        Candy!

They embrace.

CLOSE SHOT   CANDY'S FACE AND THE BACK OF CLAIRE'S HEAD

We SEE Candy's reaction of shock at the sight of Claire. As
they separate, she quickly masks it.

TWO SHOT   CANDY AND CLAIRE

                              CANDY
        I've been meaning to do this for
        ages.

                              CLAIRE
        How long has it been?

                              CANDY
        Over two years. But I guess that's
        how long it takes to catch a star.

                              CLAIRE
        Isn't it wonderful—what he's accom-
        plished?

                              CANDY
        All of us at the academy knew he'd
        do it.

                              CLAIRE
        Come, sit down.

As they do:

                              CANDY
        He believes he's so good so hard that
        others had to believe it, too.

                              CLAIRE
        He is the best.

There's a pause. Candy can't submerge her feelings.

                                                    CONTINUED

CONTINUED

> CANDY
> (lightly)
> Is the best too much of a good thing?
> You look kind of peaked, darling.

> CLAIRE
> (ruefully)
> Oh, sometimes—I guess—it gets a bit
> trying.

> CANDY
> Two years in the fast lane is a long
> time for some of us. Maybe if you
> had a line of your own.

> CLAIRE
> I just can't seem to find the time.

> CANDY
> He takes it all, doesn't he?

> CLAIRE
> He seems to need me.

> CANDY
> I know.

> CLAIRE
> I do love him.

> CANDY
> I'm sure you do. But you're no good
> at those midnight-to-dawn revels.
> Haven't you told him? Of course, it
> wouldn't do any good.

> CLAIRE
> It isn't his fault, it's mine. He's
> inexhaustible, and—I'm not.

That does it for Candy.

> CANDY
> Well—don't drown in it, pet. You're
> not the raffish type, like me. You're
> (MORE)

CONTINUED

CONTINUED

>   CANDY (CONT'D)
> a lady. And that's as hard to live
> down as a wart on the nose.
>   (rising)
> I'd better be going . . .

She rises and Claire follows.

>   CLAIRE
> But aren't you going to wait for
> Robert?

As they walk to the door.

>   CANDY
> I think not. I really came to see you.

>   CLAIRE
> He was called to the phone. He's
> talking to New York. He'll be so
> disappointed.

>   CANDY
> I daresay he'll survive. But I'd see a
> doctor if I were you. You look all
> burned out. And tell Robert from me
> to go to hell.

With a fleeting kiss on Claire's cheek, she is gone, closing the door behind her. Claire is slightly stunned by her abrupt departure. She is still trying to piece together their conversation when the door flies open and Robert bursts in. He is bubbling over. He embraces and kisses her.

>   ROBERT
> I've done it!

>   CLAIRE
> Candy just left. Didn't you see her?

>   ROBERT
> Didn't you hear me? We have it.

>   CLAIRE
> Have what?

                              CONTINUED

CONTINUED

> ROBERT
> A Hollywood movie.

Claire's reaction is less than exciting. As she dwells on it:

> ROBERT (CONT'D)
> Come along, love, we have worlds to
> conquer and times a'wasting.

> CLAIRE
> I'm not going to America with you.

> ROBERT
> Why not?

> CLAIRE
> I don't want to go to that country
> and drag around at your coat tails.

> ROBERT
> What do you want?

> CLAIRE
> Leave me behind.

> ROBERT
> Damn it, I can't! You know I won't
> leave you behind. And let's have no
> further word about it.

He storms out, slamming the door behind him.

Claire stands bleakly, contemplating her life. She wavers
and stumbles back to the dressing table. She looks into the
mirror.

PHOTO EFFECT:

As she dwells on her haggard face, it is slowly transformed
into the beauty who is now looking into the REARVIEW MIRROR.

BACK TO SCENE

Claire is looking at herself in the rearview mirror.

CONTINUED

CONTINUED

> CLAIRE
> (with a desperate effort to
> mask her delight)
> I look like a gypsy. I might at least
> be a tidy gypsy. Please give me my
> comb.

Martin fetches the comb that we last saw Claire use in Dr. Fenwick's office. As she combs her hair, he stares as if he is admiring her for the first time.

> MARTIN
> Maman was pretty, too. She had
> bright gold hair down to her waist.

> CLAIRE
> (lightly changing the subject)
> But there are other women, Mon-
> sieur Martin. There was that city
> woman whom you loved . . .

He cries out like the terrible explosion of a too-long-contained agony.

> MARTIN
> I killed her!

A deathly silence. Abruptly jarred out of her new-found complacency, Claire stares silently at Martin. Meanwhile, torn by an inner grief, his tortured eyes relive the scene. In an effort to shut out what he has just said, Claire closes her eyes. Her lips tremble and tears of pity seep through her lids. Finally, she opens her eyes to look at him again. But Martin has gone. Claire raises herself to look, bewildered, out of the open door.

FADE OUT.

FADE IN:

EXT. THE SQUARE DAY

Claire is on her bed. Next to it now is a table. She is finishing her breakfast. Martin sits on the rampart wall, his face turned silently and sadly out toward the valley.

CONTINUED

CONTINUED

Claire finishes eating and puts her bowl and plate on the table. Immediately she lies back and pretends to fall asleep. But covertly she is watching him. She feels his approach and obviously shrinks further inside herself. He bends over her. His dark eyes no longer have their secret look of preoccupation. Instead, as though aware of some change in her, he has become watchful.

> MARTIN
> Don't be afraid of me. I have done
> with killing.

> CLAIRE
> (quietly)
> I'm not afraid. Besides, what would
> be the point of it—now that you've
> made me well.

> MARTIN
> (brooding)
> If you went away from here—if you
> could—where would you go? To
> whom?

> CLAIRE
> (defensively)
> You know I've nowhere—no one.

He examines her closely with his eyes that see anew. Her fear of him becomes more evident. After a decent interval:

> MARTIN
> There are things I must do on the
> outside. I shall be gone all day.

He EXITS, moving off to the street, then on to the gully and down, until he is out of sight.

Claire continues to listen rigidly to the scuffle of his feet in the dust and gravel of the road. When they are gone, she breathes her first, unsteady sigh of relief and wipes away the sweat that has come from her tension. Still, she waits until she can hear only the sounds of the village: the tinkling of the goats' bells, the flutter of a hen's wings, the chirp of chickens.

CONTINUED

CONTINUED

Then, warily, she raises her head and looks about. She exchanges her sheet for the serape. She sits up, slides off the bed, and tries out her naked feet. She slinks over to the wall and, crouching behind it, peers over the edge to look down at the descending path.

EXT. LONG SHOT THE VALLEY DAY

Martin is crossing through the tangled growth of the ravine and slowly climbing up to the path on the other side. When he reaches the top, he is a large speck in the distance. He has a bag of produce slung over his shoulder. He turns and looks back. Then he continues on his way.

EXT. THE SQUARE DAY

Claire releases her pent-up breath. She slithers backward from the wall to a point where she can safely stand up. She flings her arms into the air and stretches in a spirit of liberated defiance. She tests her legs in short strides. They serve her so well that she does a little dance until they begin to sag, and she falls to her knees. After a moment, she raises herself to her feet again and begins to walk in measured steps toward the desolate street and the deserted, tumbled houses. Her baby goat and its mother soon trail at her heels.

EXT. THE STREET DAY

She comes to the schoolhouse and looks in the window again. As she continues, the journey turns into a painful limp. But she goes on until she comes to the door of the shattered church. She looks inside to examine the interior set of the ruin. The broken bell is shattered into pieces with the rubble of the masonry on the floor.

Claire continues and turns the corner to take the path which leads into the cemetery. The goats, having no taste for this place, disappear down the street, their bells tinkling as they go.

Claire enters the GROANING GATE and wanders among the desolate graves. At the grave of Martin's mother, Claire comes to the end of her strength. She sinks down next to the mound. A LARK SINGS; a BUTTERFLY lights on the mound

CONTINUED

CONTINUED

and then flies away. Claire runs her hand over the grave almost caressingly.

> CLAIRE
> (softly)
> I had to talk to you before I leave.
> Madame, you are wise and good.
> What is to become of me?

She waits, knowing there will be no answer.

> CLAIRE (CONT'D)
> Goodbye, Madame.

Yielding to an impulsive tenderness, Claire bends and kisses the grave.

> CLAIRE (CONT'D)
> Goodbye.

Claire rises and crosses to the gate. As she is about to leave, she stops short. Her breath catches in her throat as she senses that she is not alone. She turns to look in the direction of her suspicion.

CLAIRE'S POV: WHAT SHE SEES

Glistening above the cemetery wall are the bright yellow eyes of a goat's head with its great horns starkly etched out of the sky.

PREVIOUS SHOT   CLAIRE

Her confidence snaps; she begins to run. GO WITH HER as she stumbles and falls in her flight and then continues on.

EXT.   THE SQUARE   DAY

Stumbling and running, Claire approaches, managing to reach her bed. She falls upon it, exhausted, panting and shaken. Lying back on her bed, her strength completely gone, she closes her eyes. As she lies there, with only the sound of her deep-heaving breath—

> DISSOLVE:

EXT.   THE DESERTED STREET   NIGHT   (ON THE POSTER)

CONTINUED

CONTINUED

CAMERA is ANGLED on the lower half of the faded circus POSTER we saw in the opening.

Presently we SEE a man on the deserted street. FRAMED IN A SHOT from the hips down, he wears neat and trim trousers, smartly belted at the waist, and modern brown shoes.

PAN WITH THE LEGS as they move forward along the street. As the ANGLE WIDENS on the man's back, we can SEE that he wears a clean, white shirt that is open at the neck. Also, in the semidarkness, we can SEE that his hair is neatly trimmed, and his face is clean-shaven. When his back is in full view of the CAMERA, we can SEE that he is walking toward a modern, portable arc lamp which sits on the ground, throwing its strong beam toward the square.

The man is well-built and graceful. He picks up the lamp noiselessly and moves stealthily toward the plane tree in the square. CAMERA FOLLOWS ON HIS BACK.

When the man nears the tree, he stops. HOLD. He directs the beam of his light on Claire's bed so that we can glimpse her motionless outline as she sleeps there. Now, as he goes to her, CAMERA MOVES UP AND OVER HIS BACK. Then, at the edge of the bed, the man raises his lamp over Claire's head and looks down at her.

MAN'S POV: CLAIRE'S FACE

Part of the lamp and the man's arm may be SEEN in the SHOT.

Claire stirs in her sleep. Dimly aware of some strange presence, she slowly opens her eyes. At the sight of the man, they fill with rapid terror.

CLAIRE'S POV: THE MAN'S FACE

It is vaguely familiar with its vigorous mouth. Above the clean-shaven face, the black hair is neatly trimmed and combed. The smiling eyes have an uncertain meaning as they remain fixed on Claire. It is Martin.

TWO SHOT: CLAIRE AND MARTIN

Claire gasps hoarsely and cringes.

CONTINUED

CONTINUED

>   MARTIN
>   (shyly)
>   Here I am, Mademoiselle Claire.

Claire's heaving terror slowly settles into a mystified
voicelessness.

>   CLAIRE
>   (whispers)
>   Martin . . .

>   MARTIN
>   You see—I've had a shave and a
>   haircut. After all, a beard is an ugly
>   thing. But until you came it didn't
>   matter.

WIDE ANGLE

as Martin crosses to the tree and hooks his new lamp high
on one of the branches to spread its glow. He returns to
stand in front of Claire for inspection like an awkward boy
awaiting some approval of his appearance. Although we can
SEE some sign of Claire's uncontainable pleasure, she resists
any spoken acknowledgment. Martin tries to conceal his
disappointment.

>   MARTIN
>   I had to get a lift to Draguignan. It
>   took time, believe me. Not many
>   people will risk picking up such a
>   rough-looking fellow. Coming home
>   was easier.

He waits hopefully a moment more. But when Claire still
doesn't speak, Martin turns and disappears behind the fat
trunk of the plane tree. He reappears quickly with a paper
parcel, and unwraps it. He holds up a pink cotton quilted
coat by its shoulders.

>   MARTIN
>   (embarrassed)
>   It's called a housecoat.

CONTINUED

CONTINUED

Claire's committed silence overwhelms her emotions. Her eyes well with tears. To cover this, she lowers her glance.

CLAIRE'S POV: THE AREA BETWEEN MARTIN'S CHIN AND CHEST

The collar is open, and the gold chain and crucifix are gone. In their place, the little white line of unsunburned skin that shows where it had hung still remains.

Martin offers Claire the coat.

>   MARTIN
>   Here, put it on.

>   CLAIRE
>   (confused, stammers)
>   But, I don't want it. I never asked
>   you for it. I didn't ask you to change
>   yourself. You've lived long enough as
>   you were.

>   MARTIN
>   I know. But Maman said that some-
>   thing new might give you pleasure.
>   She said, too, that a man must make
>   himself decent for his woman.

Claire writhes under the awful presence of his kindness, knowing that she must reject it by any possible means.

>   CLAIRE
>   (with a shallow cruelty)
>   Your woman, Monsieur Martin? You
>   have a woman hidden away some-
>   where? You should have brought us
>   together.

>   MARTIN
>   (confused, simply)
>   You and Maman are the only women
>   here.
>   (with sad dignity)
>   I did not mean to offend you. I only
>   meant that you are all I have.

                                        CONTINUED

CONTINUED

Meaning to end the matter, he smiles and holds up a significant finger. Quickly, he EXITS the SHOT.

WIDE ANGLE

Martin appears from behind the tree. He is carrying the small table upon which he has already placed a new, crisp red-checkered tablecloth. In each of his hands, he holds a gay-colored plate, a mug, and a bright, shining knife and fork which he sets on the table after he has placed it near the bed. Then once more he disappears behind the tree and emerges with a covered platter, which he places on the table. He rolls the old wheelchair to the side, facing the plate.

> MARTIN
> You are to have a feast tonight.

He picks up the housecoat again, and crosses to Claire. Brooking no interference, he raises her up and puts her arms into the sleeves. Finally, Claire helps him. Pushing the sheet aside, Martin lifts Claire and sets her down gently in the chair at the table. This done, he quickly finds a small log and seats himself opposite Claire.

There is a long, uncomfortable silence. Moved as she is, Claire searches her defenses. Finally,

> CLAIRE
> (an accusation)
> You sold your gold cross and chain
> for all this, didn't you?

> MARTIN
> They belonged to Maman. Her
> mother gave it to her for her first
> communion. She said to me: "Your
> young lady is not like us. She has
> other needs." You see, she under-
> stands you better than I do. I am
> only a man. And I have been so
> much alone. I've forgotten all I knew.

He uncovers the dish. Shyly, but proudly,

CONTINUED

CONTINUED

> MARTIN (CONT'D)
> It is veal.

Claire takes a moment to examine his face.

CLAIRE'S POV: MARTIN

The rough mask that had lain behind his beard and over-grown hair is no longer there. Instead, his face is lean and strong. Now, also, his eyes have lost their brilliant, vision-ary stare. They are not any longer searching dully beyond Claire for some remote image but are looking directly and appealingly into her eyes—watching her intently.

PREVIOUS SHOT

> CLAIRE
> (artificial lightness)
> You make me think of Nanny-Anne.
> When I was ill, she used to sit beside
> me and coax me to eat. She'd say:
> "Eat your supper like a good child—
> to please me."

> MARTIN
> Did you?

> CLAIRE
> I had to. I loved her. Even at my
> naughtiest, I wanted to please her.

> MARTIN
> Please . . . please me.

Claire swallows the uncomfortable lump in her throat.

> CLAIRE
> Why not? It looks good, and I'm
> hungry. Why don't you eat with me,
> Martin?

> MARTIN
> (abashed)
> We peasants don't eat meat often.
> Not that kind of meat. Oh, a piece of
> (MORE)

CONTINUED

CONTINUED

> MARTIN (CONT'D)
> goat's flesh, perhaps. Or, on feast
> days, an old hen that would have
> died anyway. I would rather not eat
> meat at all.
>> (pause)
> But I need strength, as you do.
>> (his tension begins to mount)
> I don't want to kill. But I have to. I
> don't understand it.
>> (his voice grows harder and
>> more strained)
> I cut my pet goat's throat. A little
> calf has to die for us. Men and
> women kill each other. They don't
> know why. Afterward, they find out
> it was all a mistake. They could have
> let each other live in peace. But,
> then, it's too late.

He rubs his face roughly as if to get rid of the unpleasant
thought. He relaxes; his tension abates.

> MARTIN (CONT'D)
>> (quietly)
> Well, there it is. It must be God's
> will. Eat your meat, Mademoiselle
> Claire. Don't waste death. Grow
> strong. You are stronger. You used
> to cough your heart out. Now you
> don't cough any more.
>> (tenderly worshipful)
> You look so . . .
>> (as if he wants to say "so
>> lovely")
> . . . so young.
>> (Then, a crisp command)
> Eat.

Claire obeys. As he watches happily, he suddenly recalls
something.

CONTINUED

CONTINUED

> MARTIN
> Oh, there is one more thing.

He rises and moves off to disappear once again behind the tree. He returns with another package. He removes the contents and unfurls it like a flag for Claire.

> CLAIRE
> (touched)
> A linen sheet.

> MARTIN
> It is what you are more used to. I have brought two of each: two white shirts and two linen sheets. That way, one can be used while the other is being washed.
> (he feels the sheet appreciatively)
> It is soft. Tonight you will sleep on it.

He crosses to the bed and replaces the coarse gray sheet with the linen one.

> MARTIN (CONT'D)
> (as he busies himself)
> Today, I wasted my time buying things for only me. When I finished, it was already longer than I should have been away from you. It was too late to exchange our produce for the things we need. But tomorrow I shall leave early—long before you awake. And, I shall hurry back to you.

Claire listens stolidly, but we can see that she is torn by what she hears, and the inner workings of her mind. When she speaks, it is almost casual.

> CLAIRE
> This food is very good.

She takes a mouthful of food and chews it. But it won't go down her throat. She covers her eyes with her hand.

CONTINUED

CONTINUED

Although no sound comes from her, we can see that her
body is quaking miserably.

FADE OUT.

FADE IN:

INT.   MARTIN'S ROOM   DAY

The early morning sun bathes the empty room. After a beat,
the door is flung open, and Claire bursts in. She is wearing
the pink housecoat. Frantically, she pulls open the armoire
and removes her clothes. Item by item, she dresses in
clumsy haste. After she has slipped into her bloodstained
dress, she looks hurriedly for her shoes, but they are not to
be found. In their place, however, there is a pair of small
espadrilles. She puts them on. She snatches up her battered,
bloodstained handbag and searches quickly to verify the
contents she found there before. She removes the wallet and
looks quickly to her money. It is all there, as it was. Hurriedly she looks at her passport; it is in order. She stuffs
them back into her handbag. She goes to the door and looks
out and about carefully. Satisfied, she EXITS the room.

EXT.   MARTIN'S HOUSE   DAY

Claire ENTERS, and stands for a moment in watchful silence.
Now GO WITH HER as she hurries down the village street to
the square.

EXT.   THE SQUARE   DAY

Claire comes running into the square. She crouches low as
she approaches the retaining wall. She peers over the edge.

LONG SHOT   THE VALLEY   (CLAIRE'S POV)

CAMERA SLOWLY PANS the area. So far as the eye can see,
she sees no one. On the distant highway, an occasional car
goes by.

THE SQUARE   (ACROSS CLAIRE'S BACK)

She stands up and turns to face CAMERA, taking one last sad
and tender look at the ruined village. As she scans the area,
her eyes are held by something OS.

CONTINUED

CONTINUED

CLAIRE'S POV: THE WHEELCHAIR

HOLD FOR A BEAT, then PAN to the bed. Another PAUSE, then PAN to the spot slightly distant from the bed, where the long grass has been pressed into a mold by the weight of Martin's body.

BACK TO CLAIRE

She breaks the spell of her miserable lethargy and starts for the street.

ANGLE THE STREET (FAVORING THE SQUARE)

CAMERA IS SHOOTING FROM THE ENTRANCE TO THE VILLAGE

We SEE Claire hurrying distantly toward the CAMERA.

When she comes close enough, we can SEE the tears streaming down her cheeks; we can HEAR her tormented sobs of anguish.

CAMERA GOES WITH CLAIRE as she passes and begins her stumbling descent over the difficult path that leads down to the ravine.

LONG SHOT THE PATH (FROM BELOW)

LOOKING UP TOWARD THE VILLAGE at the point of an abrupt curve in the path.

In the distance, Claire is descending the path toward CAMERA.

The path curves around a promontory and continues down on the other side so that CAMERA can SEE Claire coming down and approaching the curve but cannot see the path as it continues on the other side of the promontory.

As Claire reaches the curve and rounds it, CAMERA TRUCKS WITH HER to reveal what is on the other side. It is Martin. A sack slung over his shoulder, his dark, sweat-drenched face is lifted to Claire in recognition of an incredible event. He measures her with the terrible intensity of a duelist in a death encounter.

Claire stands petrified. Suddenly, in a fit of unleashed fury, Martin flings his sack into the ravine. With eyes blazing

CONTINUED

CONTINUED

now, he runs toward Claire. Simultaneously, in a seemingly irrational fury, Claire runs toward Martin.

ANGLE A SECTION OF THE PATH BETWEEN MARTIN AND CLAIRE

For a moment, the SHOT is empty. Then, hurtling into FRAME, Claire and Martin collide. As she strikes and claws violently at Martin's panting, straining body, he picks her up in his arms as he has done so many times before. Only this time we can SEE rage and hunger in his face as Claire lays her nails against him, tearing his white shirt and goring his shoulder.

In the end, their mutual savagery is brief. For, under the turmoil, there is the deep-seated need for release from this long and hopeless struggle.

INT. MARTIN'S ROOM DAY

Martin ENTERS and flings his package down on the bed. The shutters are drawn and the light subdued. Then, frenzied in the half light, he tears away each item of her clothing, piece by piece, until she lies naked beneath him. Driven by the furious search of his suddenly wild desire, Martin lays the burden of his panting body on Claire. And now, in an equally furious exaltation, Claire embraces Martin.

FADE OUT.

FADE IN:

EXT. THE SQUARE DAY

The ANGLE is across Martin's profile in FG as he sits on the rampart wall overlooking the valley. His face holds the inner ravages of his conscience from the earlier event. But we can also detect a sharply different presence of mind and an austere peace. He is freshly shaved and wears a clean shirt.

In BG, we SEE Claire approaching. Her face and hair are neatly composed but her figure is different. She is wearing Martin's mother's black dress. It fits her well. The austere bodice has been buttoned up neatly, but, although the skirt hangs decently, it reaches down to her ankle. With her

CONTINUED

CONTINUED

handbag tucked under her arm, she stands waiting for
Martin to turn to her. When he does, he is slightly startled.

>   MARTIN
>   I thought for a moment you were my
>   mother.

Claire runs her hand over the dress.

>   CLAIRE
>   Do you mind? Would she have
>   minded?

>   MARTIN
>   She would have wanted you to wear
>   it. She was a careful woman. She did
>   not like things to be wasted.

Claire seats herself on the wall, facing Martin. For a long
moment, she studies his face.

>   CLAIRE
>   You know your mother is dead—
>   don't you, Martin?

CLOSE   MARTIN

His eyes are brilliant, but they are calm eyes—bereft of the
last sheltering illusion. He shrugs slightly as if to say,
"What can one do?"

>   MARTIN
>   Yes.

TWO SHOT   CLAIRE AND MARTIN

>   CLAIRE
>   This morning when you found me—
>   why did you come back, Martin? Did
>   you guess?

>   MARTIN
>   No. I didn't want you to think that
>   of me. I came back because I heard
>   that government men were at
>   Draguignan. It's just as you said:
>   (MORE)

CONTINUED

CONTINUED

> MARTIN (CONT'D)
> they are coming here. You are a
> foreigner—they might make things
> difficult.

> CLAIRE
> If they find you, Martin—will they
> take you away?

> MARTIN
> Why should they do that?

> CLAIRE
> (faltering)
> You said—once—you killed some-
> one—a woman . . .

> MARTIN
> (wearily)
> That was a long time ago. In those
> days people often killed each other.
> Sometimes for the right, sometimes
> for the wrong—sometimes for no
> reason. No one cared very much. No
> one cares now. No one remembers.

> CLAIRE
> No one knows you killed her?

> MARTIN
> I know. I loved her. I had never
> loved anyone before.

> CLAIRE
> (suddenly urgent)
> Help me to understand, Martin. I
> must.

Martin rises.

> MARTIN
> Soon you will be gone—back to your
> people. It is better if you do not wait.
> I will take you to the highway . . .

CONTINUED

CONTINUED

> CLAIRE
> I can't go away from here not know-
> ing.

> MARTIN
> (dodging)
> But you must be careful whom you
> ride with. You must look at the face
> well.

> CLAIRE
> I will. But . . .

> MARTIN
> (overriding)
> Come. The road is hard from here. It
> will take time.

From old habit, he starts to help her. But as she rises, he
quickly realizes she doesn't need him. He withdraws his
hand awkwardly. In his embarrassment, he pretends to be
amused. As they go . . .

> MARTIN
> My mother's dress will not become
> you where you are going.

> CLAIRE
> I'm sure the citizens of Draguignan
> will not pay particular attention.

> MARTIN
> They might even think you to be one
> of them.

> CLAIRE
> I still have some money. I'm told
> they have a smart couteriere.

As they pass the tower and onto the street that leads down
to the ravine, Martin stops abruptly and turns to Claire.

> MARTIN
> (as though he has long been
> suppressing it)
> Forgive me.

CONTINUED

CONTINUED

>   CLAIRE
> Martin—I'm not a child to forgive
> anyone.

He seems satisfied, and they start to walk again. As they go,

>   CLAIRE
>   (protesting)
> I can't go away from here not know-
> ing. I've told you all I know about
> myself—the wrong, stupid, weak
> things. Tell me. We have so little
> time.

The walking seems to have an unwinding effect on him.

>   MARTIN
> All right.
>   (it is not easy)
> The war broke loose when I was 18.
> At first, it stayed a long way off.
> But, one day, our cure was arrested.
> For the first time, we learned France
> was conquered.

Claire stumbles and falls. Martin quickly helps her to her
feet.

>   MARTIN
> Are you hurt?

>   CLAIRE
> My ankle. I turned it a little. Could I
> rest a minute?

Martin points to a large rock.

>   MARTIN
> Sit there.

Claire sits, and Martin crouches beside her.

>   CLAIRE
> What happened after that?

                                              CONTINUED

CONTINUED

>   MARTIN
> It was terrible to be hunted not only
> by the enemy but by one's own
> people—to be able to trust no one.
>   (as if in a dream)
> One day, at a meeting of the cell, my
> father was killed and I was wounded.
> With one other man, I managed to
> escape. But he was dying and he
> entrusted me with the names of
> those who were still unsuspected—
> with whom I could find refuge, and
> perhaps rebuild our forces.
>   (rubs his face roughly)
> It is not worth telling.

>   CLAIRE
> Please, Martin, you don't under-
> stand. It's more than just a story
> to me—it means my life—it means
> what I am, where I'm going, what I
> will do.

>   MARTIN
> My wound was worsening, but I
> managed to make my way to a small
> town where I could find one of the
> names I had been given. I knocked a
> signal at the door, and when it was
> opened by a girl, I fell half-dead into
> her arms.

>   CLAIRE
> And that was the girl?

>   MARTIN
> Constance.
>   (he looks up into the sky)
> The sun is moving rapidly. It will
> grow much hotter. If you are rested,
> we should walk.

CONTINUED

CONTINUED

CLAIRE
All right.

Martin rises and helps Claire to her feet. They continue.

CLAIRE
This Constance—did she help you?

MARTIN
She brought me to her bed and
undressed me. I learned from her
that men and women are alike in
their needs and suffering. Each day,
she went to work so no one would
suspect she was sheltering me. Then,
under cover of darkness, she would
tend to my wounds and my needs.

CLAIRE
She was very brave.

MARTIN
She lived in deadly fear. I told her:
"You are risking your life." She said:
"What else can I do?" When I was
afraid I would die, I told her the
names that had been given to me.
She pleaded with me not to; I told
her she was the only one I could
trust—that she had to know. She told
me that her mother and father had
been shot as hostages.

At this point, they have reached the ravine. Martin looks
down into the gully and points.

MARTIN
That is where I found you.

Claire looks down.

LONG SHOT INTO THE GULLY (CLAIRE'S POV)

We can SEE the remains of Claire's shattered car, now oblit-
erated by the foliage that has grown over and around it.

CONTINUED

CONTINUED

> MARTIN
> Come. This will not be easy.

He lifts her in his arms and starts to penetrate the gully.

> MARTIN
> You must look to the briers, they are
> very sharp.

Using all his effort, he negotiates the gully with Claire.

ANGLE THE SMALL RUTTED ROAD

He comes over the edge with Claire in his arms. Panting
deeply, he sets her down and kneels on the road.

> CLAIRE
> You shouldn't have done that. I could
> have walked.

> MARTIN
> It would be too much for such small
> feet.

Claire sits on the road beside Martin and waits, unable to
take her eyes from the face of this tragic man. Presently,

> CLAIRE
> Was she beautiful?

> MARTIN
> Like you. Only she was fair. Her hair
> was a bright gold. Her eyes were as
> blue as yours.

> CLAIRE
> When did you become lovers?

> MARTIN
> I can't remember. There was so great
> hunger, so great terror—it was only
> natural, I suppose, that love—when
> it came—should also be great.

Martin gets to his feet, helping Claire up. They start walking
along the path, CAMERA LEADING them. Martin walks in silence,
lost in his thoughts. But Claire cannot bear the silence.

CONTINUED

CONTINUED

> CLAIRE
> When did it happen?

> MARTIN
> Happen?

Claire translates the question in her eyes. Martin
understands.

> MARTIN
> Oh. There came a night when the
> rifle butts knocked on the house
> door. We could hear the heavy boots
> on the naked stairs. It was a familiar
> sound.
> (he mimics the Nazi image)
> Open up! Open up there! Constance
> turned to me. I had not seen such
> terror before. She said, "Martin—I'm
> not like you—I cannot bear pain." I
> tried to quiet her. I said, "It is me
> they are after, they will not hurt
> you." But, she cried, "The names—
> you have told me the names."

From this point on, Martin's anger begins to seethe, and his
voice rises as he starts to relive the whole episode.

> MARTIN (CONT'D)
> I said they needn't know. She said:
> "But I do—and when I'm hurt and
> frightened, I'll do anything, say
> anything. Terrible things. It was I
> who betrayed my father and mother.
> The officer said, "'If you don't tell me
> where they are, we shall know how
> to deal with you!'" He burned her
> breast with his lighted cigarette.
> (the memory is too much for
> him; he is crying loudly)
> She told him everything. She pleaded
> and cried to me: "Martin—if these
> (MORE)

CONTINUED

CONTINUED

> MARTIN (CONT'D)
> men come again I shall tell them
> everything. You mustn't let me! I
> could not go on living!"

Martin realizes that he has been shouting at the top of his
lungs. He sags, and with the back of his hand he wipes the
corners of his eyes. Recovering, he continues quietly.

> MARTIN
> I looked into her eyes. They were
> scarcely human with terror. She
> knew I kept a revolver under my
> pillow. She seized it and forced it into
> my hand. She whispered, "They're
> here now—you must not wait . . ."
> (beat)
> And then the gun went off—and she
> was dead.

Claire falls to her knees and remains kneeling. For the first
time, she cries convulsively and uncontrollably. Martin,
standing erect, turns away to look out over the highway and
the hills.

EXT. THE SMALL RUTTED ROAD (ABOUT 100 YARDS FROM THE
HIGHWAY) DAY

Claire and Martin are approaching the camera. We can see
the occasional car passing. Like the sobs that remain in a
child's breast long after she has cried her heart out, Claire
is reaching the end.

> CLAIRE
> I'm sorry I behaved so badly, Martin.
> Forgive me.

> MARTIN
> As you say, I am not one to forgive.

> CLAIRE
> Have you been thinking about her all
> this time?

CONTINUED

CONTINUED

> MARTIN
> I don't know. After that, something
> went wrong inside my head. The
> police took me—I was shut up with
> other crazy men. It was not pleasant.
> Then, one day—after a year or two, I
> suppose—I escaped. I found my way
> home. As you saw, there was no one
> left—except Maman, who had waited
> for me.

> CLAIRE
> And she took care of you.

> MARTIN
> When she was dying, she told me not
> to be afraid. She said she would never
> really leave me—and that some day
> some other woman would come to
> take her place.

They have now come to the intersection of the highway.

> MARTIN (CONT'D)
> And now, you are leaving.
> (sadly)
> It is best that you do.

> CLAIRE
> (reassuring him)
> You were good to me, Martin—you
> gave me something more than life—
> you gave me the will to live.
> (gently)
> Perhaps I was an atonement.

> MARTIN
> Perhaps at first—but, then it was for
> you—even though you hated me.

> CLAIRE
> It wasn't hatred. Only a stupid resent-
> ment because you made me live when
> I so much wanted to die. But I'm
> grateful now . . . humbly grateful.

EXT. THE HIGHWAY DAY

Now the cars are more frequent.

> MARTIN
>
> When I saw you on that path—
> upright, free—I forgot that I had no
> right to you—or to any woman.

> CLAIRE
>
> That's foolishness, Martin. All that
> sorrow is in the past. She under-
> stood—as I do. If she had betrayed
> you and your friends as she knew
> she would, she couldn't have endured
> and gone on living.

She takes his hand and, with the other, turns his face to
hers.

> CLAIRE (CONT'D)
>
> You took a life, and you saved a life.
> The death is canceled.

Slowly, the understanding filters into Martin's mind. He
smiles.

> MARTIN
>
> You must have laughed at me. All
> the things I did for you—you could
> have done them for yourself.

> CLAIRE
>
> Not at first—not for a long time.

> MARTIN
>
> You should have told me when you
> didn't need me anymore.

> CLAIRE
>
> I was afraid. I thought if you knew,
> you wouldn't let me go.

> MARTIN
>
> Well, now you're free. I will not wait
> here with you while . . .
>> (he gestures his meaning)
>> (MORE)

CONTINUED

CONTINUED

> MARTIN (CONT'D)
> . . . it would seem strange for a man
> to be with you at such a time.

Claire doesn't have an answer. Martin continues awkwardly.

> MARTIN
> What kind of a man could he be?

> CLAIRE
> (a note of finality)
> A fine man. A wonderful man.

> MARTIN
> Though you don't need me any-
> more—still, if you can't sleep, or
> should you be afraid, I shall still
> hear you.

> CLAIRE
> Goodbye, Martin.

She draws his mouth to hers. It is a sisterly kiss. Martin does not embrace her. Claire turns quickly, and hurries to the border of the highway. Martin watches her a moment, then turns and starts back along the path to the deserted village.

MARTIN

As he walks, he swallows hard. Slowly his eyes well up. He reaches into his new trousers and takes out a cloth with which he wipes his eyes. He puts the cloth back in his pocket.

WIDE ANGLE

To INCLUDE the INTERSECTION BEHIND MARTIN

As Martin strides toward the camera, a small open car is seen to turn off the highway and onto the dirt path. It proceeds toward the camera until Martin can HEAR its SOUND behind him. Martin turns and waits for it to pull up along-side him. The car bumps along and comes to a stop.

ANGLE THE OPEN CAR AND ITS OCCUPANTS

CONTINUED

CONTINUED

Behind the wheel and driving is the starchily correct Parisian intellectual whom we saw earlier as FOURTH MAN. Sitting next to him is the heavy-shouldered old painter who was FIRST MAN. FOURTH MAN makes a stiff little bow to Martin and removes his pince-nez. With an immaculate handkerchief, he rubs away the film of dust.

ANOTHER ANGLE   TO INCLUDE MARTIN

> FOURTH MAN
> I represent the Ministry of Fine Arts.
> We have a scheme afoot to rehabili-
> tate some of our country's historic
> villages. My good friend Monsieur
> Bernard has persuaded me that this
> is one of them.

Martin looks blankly at the man, his mind utterly removed from anything he has said.

> FIRST MAN
> (to Fourth Man)
> Please—there is first an important
> question.
> (to Martin)
> Do you live up there? In the village?

Martin, at a loss, looks up at the village. Then,

> FOURTH MAN
> Well, you see, we would like to . . . er
> . . . endeavor to rebuild the village
> with proper amenities and encourage
> the former owners to return to their
> fields and vineyards.

CAMERA RISES to INCLUDE the long stretch of rutted road behind the car. In BG we can SEE Claire hurriedly walking toward the car.

> FOURTH MAN (CONT'D)
> We hope also that artists and for-
> eigners will lend a hand as they have
> done at Perouges and elsewhere.

CONTINUED

CONTINUED

Martin sees Claire approaching.

> FIRST MAN
> (to Martin)
> Presumably you have some sort of
> living quarters up there.

> MARTIN
> What?

> FOURTH MAN
> (to First Man)
> What's wrong with this man?

Claire reaches the car; she comes up and stands beside
Martin.

> CLAIRE
> May I help you?

> FOURTH MAN
> (at the end of his tether)
> As far as my breath allows, I have
> been trying to explain to Monsieur
> here . . .

> FIRST MAN
> (to Claire)
> What's his name?

> CLAIRE
> (hotly)
> His name? Why don't you ask him?

> FOURTH MAN
> (same)
> We have been try . . .

FIRST MAN puts a restraining hand on his arm.

> FIRST MAN
> (to Martin)
> What is your name, Monsieur?

> MARTIN
> (vigorously)
> Martin Thibaut.

CONTINUED

CONTINUED

> FIRST MAN
> (rummaging in his mind)
> Thibaut . . . Thibaut . . .
> (suddenly a delightful rumi-
> nation)
> Ah, yes, of course. Auberge Au
> Chant des Alouettes. I remember it
> well. In my day, it was an inn—a
> famous little inn—two-starred in
> Michelin.

FOURTH MAN beams delightedly.

> FIRST MAN
> It must have been your grand-
> mother, Monsieur, who made it
> famous with her piperade. And then,
> no doubt, your mother.

Martin and Claire smile warmly at the recollection.

> MARTIN
> It was my mother.

> FOURTH MAN
> Well, we have all had hard times.
> But, like your village, we're made of
> stubborn stuff. We can be knocked
> about, but we survive.

FIRST MAN looks up at the rise and the desiccated village.

> FIRST MAN
> Strange, how quickly human dwell-
> ings fall in ruins when the human
> heart has deserted them. And how
> quickly they are reborn with love.

> FOURTH MAN
> (sanguinely)
> Just waiting for the right hands to
> get to work.

He looks up at the rise, too.

CONTINUED

CONTINUED

>   FOURTH MAN
> A superb view of the valley. People
> who love France for what she was,
> and still is, will come back here.

>   FIRST MAN
> Yes. I even remember the old sign
> over your door. Auberge Au Chant
> des Alouettes. A charming name. But
> a crude painting. In my senility I
> could do better.

He looks at Claire with absolutely no sign of recognition.

>   FIRST MAN (CONT'D)
> I might paint a new sign for you,
> Madame.

>   FOURTH MAN
> A delightful patronne.

>   FIRST MAN
>   (with his special eye for
>   beauty)
> Indeed, indeed—
>   (to Claire)
> That is, if indeed you live here, too.

TWO SHOT   CLAIRE AND MARTIN

Martin lowers his eyes to avoid an embarrassment. Claire,
in turn, appears to dwell on the question.

>   LORD SERRAT'S
>   VOICE (OS)
> Build your own house, my child.
> Don't count on us—on what we've
> been—oneself is all one really has.

>   CLAIRE
>   (smiling gravely)
> Yes—I belong here, too.

She turns and meets Martin's incredulous smile, then turns
back to the FIRST MAN.

                                        CONTINUED

CONTINUED

> CLAIRE (CONT'D)
> Would you care to have us show you
> around?

> FOURTH MAN
> But, of course.

> CLAIRE
> (with her new-found
> strength)
> Martin, the door, please.

Beside himself with exquisite joy, Martin scrambles to the
back door of the car and jerks it open. He helps Claire in,
gets in himself, and slams the door shut. Claire smiles
calmly at Martin. As the car goes bumping forward along
the rutted road, she takes his hand and links his arm
closely with hers.

> FADE OUT.

THE END

Part 3

QUESTIONING YOUR ADAPTATION

QUESTIONING YOUR ADAPTATION

The following part of our study is designed to help you reconsider the elements of your play that make it work. To be able to assess your own efforts, especially in an area as elusive as art, is not always easy. Just as a mathematician proves his arithmetic, so a screenwriter may prove a script by carefully answering these questions.

This exercise certainly may serve simply as the catalyst for a hasty final revision for some writers. But this investigation will provide a greater degree of understanding in the nuances and shadings of dramatic art for those who are more purposeful about their skill in writing for the screen.

Most qualified professional writers acknowledge that a script has never been written which cannot be improved by cutting. We will presume, therefore, that you will make every effort to trim the script wherever possible.

Ask yourself:

Q. At the very outset, did you confront the audience with a character who is already involved or is about to become involved in *trouble*? If not, is the situation at least troublesome? Or, at the very least, does the situation promise that trouble lies ahead?

Q. Is the protagonist about to make some move or arrive at some decision which will become a turning point in his or her life (the *point of departure*)?

Q. Does your protagonist appeal to the emotions of the audience (*sympathy, empathy, antipathy*)?

Q. Does the *problem* emerge soon and clearly? Does it present a human challenge? Is there at least one person whose emotions are being tested?

Q. Have you *oriented* the audience to the information that it needs to know in order clearly to understand your story?

Q. Have you handled your *exposition* in a manner that would make the audience eager to have the information?

Q. If you have used a *flashback*, does it move the action of the story forward?

Q. Do matters *deteriorate* or *worsen* as the protagonist attempts to salvage the situation?

Q. Have you considered any of the following devices that contribute to gaining the *attention* of the audience: (a) Presenting a situation with which the audience is unfamiliar: a strange or novel experience, an extraordinary location or setting, an unusual or mystifying event? (b) Presenting a commonplace or familiar situation which is shared by the audience? (This is most effective when the experience evokes in the viewer a reaction such as, "You know, that very same thing happened to me!") (c) Presenting a character who is odd, unusual, or striking.

Q. Overall, does the opening of your play suddenly illuminate an ongoing story at a *crucial* and *emotional* moment?

Q. Have you created an emotional response in the audience by generating a sense of *sympathy* or *empathy* for your protagonist?

Q. Have you established an *intimate relationship* with the characters?

Q. Do matters *worsen* when the protagonist attempts to salvage the situation?

Q. Does the *opposing force* grow stronger as the play progresses? Does the antagonist create a *need* for *increasingly crucial decisions* by the protagonist, thus effecting greater *suspense*?

Q. Does the *issue of conflict* have great significance for the protagonist?

Q. Does the problem develop through a succession of *culminating events*?

Q. Are the main characters *unique* and *original*?

Q. Are the *values* and *traits* of your protagonist always consistent?

Q. Does the *plot* ever call for a *decision* by any character that is inconsistent with that character's previously held *values*?

Q. Do the *characters* concern themselves *exclusively* with the *problem* of the play?

Q. Does each successive *event* grow out of the preceding *event*, and does each one *culminate* at its highest point of *action*?

Q. Does each *development* peak in a further *intensification* of the *clash* between the *problem* and the *conflict*?

Q. Do your disclosures constantly create increasing *suspense*? In other words, do you parcel them out in small doses and at regular intervals, withholding full knowledge until the play is almost over; that is, keeping audience *anticipation* at fever pitch?

Q. Do you continually heighten the interest in your characters by creating additional *sympathy, empathy,* or *antipathy* for them?

Q. Will the audience worry and be increasingly curious about how the *problem* will come out in the end?

Q. Does the uncertainty of the outcome continue to increase audience *anxiety* right up to the *climax* of the play?

Q. Is the result of the *final decision* constantly suspended until the end of the play?

Q. If the *goal* is obvious, does your *suspense* grow out of the question: How will the conclusion be reached in view of all the seemingly impossible obstacles?

Q. Have you found moments for minor suspense?

Q. Have you used the technique of developing *expectancy* only to reverse it for *surprise*?

Q. Have you used *expectancy* in the promise of a *confrontation* between two adversaries? If so, have you fulfilled that obligation? In other words, have you established expectancy for any *obligatory* scene?

Q. Have you diminished the play by *oversimplifying* or *overexplaining*?

Q. Have you flattered the intelligence of your audience by allowing them to draw conclusions from your *implications*?

Q. Is there any part of your play where you *talk* about the *action* rather than *reveal* it? (Note: The audience cannot agonize over vital decisions that are merely referred to. Characters must *live* through their *problems*.)

Q. Does the audience *feel* the basic *conflict, crisis,* and *climax*?

Q. Is there the slightest semblance of anything that strains *plausibility, believability,* or *credibility*?

Q. Have you *prepared* the audience in advance for developments or facts that may appear to be *unreasonable, remote,* or *unbelievable*?

Q. Have you activated at every opportunity the *violence* in your play?

Q. Have you religiously avoided *gratuitous violence* or *brutality* for its own sake?

Q. Is there a steady progression of *anticipation* and *anxiety*, or do certain scenes *wander aimlessly* without furthering the action?

Q. Do you have enough *complications* to insure a *steady rise* in the growing emotional *tension* of the story?

Q. Does each *scene* end with a focused, forceful *speech*? Does dialogue sound like everyday *conversation*?

Q. Does each *act* end with a *major development* that creates *suspense* and *expectancy*?

Q. Does the story reach a satisfying *climax*? Will the audience feel pleased or rewarded for having attended?

Q. Does the *plot* contain any extraneous or unnecessary developments that do not relate to the problem?

Q. Have you given the characters added dimension through *mannerisms*?

Q. Does your script throw all the *characters* into sharp relief? Would the *dialogue* of one *character* be unbecoming in the mouth of another?

Q. Does every *speech* of the play clearly *motivate* the next? Does every *scene* motivate the next?

Q. Are all the *changes* in *time* and *location* crystal clear?

Q. Have you carefully indicated the placement and movement of the *camera* to cover all dramatic nuances and touches which you believe are necessary, while, at the same time, avoiding unnecessary and arty *camera angles and shots* which impair readability and suggest unprofessionalism?

RECAP

The very first consideration in adapting a story (apart from your very strong feeling in favor of it) is: What amount of material can be covered in conventional dramatic form as compared to other literary forms? In television, particularly, the time period is rigidly and inflexibly controlled. Even in the most expanded motion picture form, the length of a screenplay is clearly limited.

Consequently, a dramatic adaptation of a story is first and foremost a shortening or cutting process: removing scenes and characters without damaging the story. In the best sense, an adaptation improves the story. Since an adapter cannot excise individual characters and scenes without affecting the overall plot and purpose, the project is inevitably reduced to a wholesale revision of the entire story: an original screenplay.

One simple technique for cutting stories which are dramatically overweight is in removing the subplots. This means, of course, that the adapter must also remove any references to the subplots wherever they occur in the plot.

The second most reasonable place to trim a story involves eliminating characters who are not vital to the plot, or merging several characters into one who can do the job of all. And, finally, a story can be cut by telescoping long scenes which usually destroy the pace of the play.

Above all, the adapter should not try to crowd in all the facts from the longer story. What will be central to the play is the original author's point of view for the story. In short, what is the basic subtext the author intended to convey?

In almost all cases, most of the material in a story is told by the author, rather than being presented in the form of dialogue between the characters. Indeed, some stories have no dialogue at all. When that is the case, the dramatist is obliged to translate the meaning by creating dialogue which contains the spirit and flavor that characterize the story.

Additionally, this kind of storytelling involves large doses of exposition. Here again, the dramatist is responsible for avoiding expository speeches, substituting action, and maintaining the realistic quality of everyday conversation.

Of course, a certain amount of exposition is necessary, especially where the original story spends a good deal of time at the outset introducing characters as the plot slowly unravels. The dramatist, as we have come to realize, cannot afford that kind of luxury if he or she is to hold onto the audience. Therefore, the adapter must start the play with an exciting development that may not occur in the original story until the reader is well into it. After that, the audience must receive the needed information by way of exposition which artfully provokes a sense of suspense either because one person needs to tell it or another person needs to hear it.

Also, more often than not, dialogue lifted straight from the original story will not work in play form. Even less likely is the chance that the speeches from the original will contain all the elements that are required for good play dialogue. Add to that the fact that the interchanges will invariably be too long and need to be broken up. Despite all of these probabilities, an adapter must judiciously avoid mangling a perfectly good speech in the story.

Most important is the objective of maintaining the original spirit of the story: your reason for choosing it. This includes the need to construct speeches that are indistinguishable from the style and quality of the original work.

In selecting a story for adaptation, avoid those where you are able to determine in advance that the effectiveness of the material depends for its success on the medium in which it was originally presented. In the final analysis, some stories defy any translation that sustains their original spirit, purpose, and mood. You should especially be wary of stories that do not lend themselves to a willing suspension of disbelief. Get to know the original material as intimately as if you had created it yourself. By that, I mean for you to get to know your story as intimately as I got to know I.A.R. Wylie's *Claire Serrat*: the characters and their values, traits, and mannerisms; the plot structure with its issues of conflict, crisis, and climax; and finally, the theme, which is the essence or totality of the play.

When you have done all of this and have decided that the story will translate well, then you should follow the same steps you would take if you were creating your own play, which, in fact, you are doing. To repeat what we said at the beginning: an adaptation is an original screenplay and, as such, it is entitled to its own copyright protection. After you have secured the necessary copyright permissions, you are ready to begin your creative work.

First, set forth the premise of the story in three short paragraphs which describe its beginning, middle, and end.

Second, determine at what point in the original story the play is going to open — your point of departure. Then, create a backstory of the principal characters, describing what took place in their lives before the play started.

Third, write a treatment of the story in the present tense. Don't *tell* the story. Instead, describe what happens in terms of characters' actions; that is, what they say and what they do as it relates to cause and effect.

Then, write the teleplay or screenplay.

Finally, "prove" your script by questioning every aspect of its construction with the questions we have provided.

With good luck and good fortune, this may be your most exciting adventure.

GLOSSARY OF
FILM TERMS

ACTION—1. The development of conflict in a scene and screenplay; 2. the function of movement that takes place in the camera's view; 3. the emotional content of a line reading, usually found in parentheses under the character's name.

ANIMATION—The movement of inanimate objects, such as cutouts or puppets, photographed one frame at a time in order to create the impression of action; also used to describe action that is drawn by an artist instead of live.

ANSWER PRINT—The first print of a finished film that combines audio, sound effects, optical effects, and music in a form that is ready to be released.

ART DIRECTOR—The set designer; frequently relied on for choosing locations.

AUDIO—The sound portion of a motion picture.

BACKGROUND (BG)—Sound or properties that are distant from the camera in any given shot.

BACK LIGHT— A light thrown from the rear of the set to give an impression of depth.

BACK LOT—Exterior portion of a studio that contains streets and the facades of buildings commonly used in motion pictures.

BEAT—A significant pause; a momentary increment of time.

BLIMP—Housing in which a camera is placed to muffle the sound of its motor.

BLOWUP—An enlarged film image produced by a laboratory optical process.

BOOM—A mount used to project a microphone or camera over a set. *See also* DOLLY.

BUSINESS—Description of the movements of the actors in a scene; usually contained in paragraphs written below shots.

CAPER—An adventure film in which characters plot to achieve a goal, as in planning a robbery.

CLOSE SHOT (CS)—This is not to be confused with a close-up. It is a close angle of two or more elements close to the viewer.

CLOSE-UP (CU)—This shot focuses clearly on a single object in a scene, either a person or an object. *See also* EXTREME CLOSE-UP.

COMPOSITE—A single piece of film with corresponding sound and images.

COMPOSITION—The balance of the artistic elements of a picture.

CONFRONTATION—A moment of conflict in which one force or character tries to reach an immediate goal and the opposing force or character poses an obstacle to it.

CONTINUITY—A comprehensive description of the complete action, scenes, dialogue, and other screenplay elements in the order in which they are to be shown on the screen.

CONTRAST—Creating a comparison of explicit difference in lighting objects or areas for dramatic effect.

CRANE—A type of camera boom.

CREDIT—Any title that acknowledges the contribution of a person to a film.

CURTAIN LINE—The closing speech in an act.

CUT—An instantaneous transition from one shot to the next by splicing the two shots to each other.

CUTAWAY—A form of continuity cutting most discernible in a point of view shot: for example, a character opens a desk drawer and looks in; the following shot shows a gun in the drawer.

CUTBACK—The shot that follows the cutaway.

CUTTER—*See* EDITOR.

CUTTING—An edited film version of a script designed to maintain a continuous flow of action.

CYCLORAMA—A semicircular backdrop behind a set.

DAY FOR NIGHT—Shooting exterior shots in the daytime with a filter to achieve the appearance of night; when a nighttime shot is actually shot at night, it is called "night for night."

DENOUEMENT—Another word for the resolution of the plot.

DEUS EX MACHINA—A contrived device used to resolve a problem; a condition that arises when a writer tries to play God and bring something to pass in the play that defies all logic or naturalness and for which the audience has not been prepared.

DISSOLVE—An optical effect of bringing a picture in while collaterally fading the previous picture out.

DOLLY—A wheeled mount upon which a camera is placed for ensuring the smooth movement of the camera within the area of the shot. *See also* BOOM.

DOLLYING—The movement of the camera on its dolly toward or away from its subject.

DOWN—Reducing the volume of sound (decibel level).

DUB—The application of sounds to the film that were not recorded at the same time the film was shot.

EDITOR—The individual who brings together all the film that has been shot into one composition by selecting, arranging, cutting, and splicing and whose aim is to make the best picture.

EFFECTS—1. Sound effects: separately recorded sounds applied to the film as needed; 2. special effects: visual effects created in the laboratory through animation or other processes.

ESTABLISH (EST)—Shot made to communicate the total atmosphere of a scene or sequence; usually indicated when the settings are complex and contain a number of points of interest.

EXPOSITION—Revealing material that is commonly referred to as the backstory.

EXTREME CLOSE-UP (ECU)—This is simply a tighter close-up in which a specific object or feature, such as the eyes or mouth of an individual or a ring on someone's finger, is the subject.

FADE—An optical effect in which the light dims: Fade out is dimming to complete darkness; fade in goes from a blank screen to a full picture.

FAVORING—Selects the character to be favored in the shot.

FLASHBACK—A shot or sequence that reveals something that occurred in the past.

FOCUS—Achieving sharpness or fuzziness of an image.

FOLLOW—A shot in which the camera follows an individual or specific action as requested.

FOREGROUND (FG)—Voices or properties that appear nearest the camera in a given shot.

FRAME—To arrange the composition of a single picture on a strip of motion picture film; a *frame* is a single picture.

FREEZE FRAME—To hold one image on a strip of motion picture film by repeating the single frame.

FULL SHOT—This angle is taken at a considerable distance and is used to establish the entire scene for the purpose of orientation.

GAFFER—The chief electrician, whose job is to light the sets as the first camera operator designates.

GAG—A stunt set up by professional stuntmen.

GIMMICK—A device that is uniquely employed to help solve a problem situation.

GRIP—A stagehand who moves and repairs the properties that are used in the shooting of a picture.

GROUP SHOT—A shot that includes four or more characters in the action.

HAND HELD—An effect in which the camera is physically held and moved by the camera operator; the resulting jerky motion, similar to that in newsreel footage, is often used to create an on-the-spot sense of reality.

HEAD-ON SHOT—Straight into the camera.

HIGH ANGLE—When the camera shoots down from above the subject.

HIGH-KEY LIGHTING—When the main light isolates an area that is contrasted sharply and brilliantly with the rest of the set.

HOOK—An incident in the opening of a picture that is used to capture audience attention.

INKY-DINK—A small incandescent lamp that is used to spotlight something.

INSERT—A shot, usually close, of an item, done separately and later inserted into the picture.

JEOPARDY—When the complexion of circumstances is threatening to a character.

JUMP CUT—An effect of jerkiness achieved when a film is spliced so as to leave a gap in what should be continuous movement; sometimes it is the result of negligence or, sometimes, by design because of too little film; it generally occurs when there is a cut in the film that interrupts the action without a corresponding change of camera angle.

KEY LIGHT—The main source of light in a shot.

LAP DISSOLVE—A laboratory process in which one shot fades out as the next fades in.

LEAD—The protagonist or central character.

LIGHTING SETUP—The gaffer's layout or plan to supply all the necessary setups of shots with the needed light; a major shooting expense.

LIMBO—A shot that has no physical connection with a set or appears to be in space.

LIP SYNC—Dialogue synchronization in which an actor, separately from the shooting of the film, utters the speech by matching it to the filmed lip movements; usually required when the original scene was shot under conditions that made the audio unusable and the lip sync sound is subsequently dubbed in.

LOCATION—A real exterior or interior setting rather than a staged set or the back lot; off the studio lot.

LONG SHOT (LS)—This angle differs from a full shot: though taken from the same long distance of the viewer from the subject, the LS shows only the portion of the scene that the audience is specifically meant to see.

LOOP—A strip of film that is so spliced it can be projected continuously; a loop is frequently used in dubbing (looping) sessions in which actors may be required to repeat their lines over and over in order to lip sync them properly.

LOW ANGLE—When the camera shoots up from below.

MACRO SHOT—An extreme close-up that outlines a small, critical detail in the action.

MAIN TITLE—The listing at the opening of a picture that includes the title and the main contributors to the production.

MATCHING—The necessity that all the elements of a scene remain constant from shot to shot: for example, if an actor is wearing a tie in one shot, it must be there in the next unless we see him remove it; customarily the duty of the script supervisor.

MATCHING SHOT—A transition in which a shot is dissolved to a successive shot that has the same character of composition (e.g., a shot of a running faucet dissolves to a shot of a waterfall).

MATTE—1. A shot in which a background is painted in; 2. the term *mask* is also used when an optical printer is used to simulate the kind of view that is effected, such as through a keyhole or binoculars.

MEDIUM SHOT (MS or MED. SHOT)—This angle is neither long nor close; a middle distance from the subject.

MINIATURE—A small-scale rendition of the physical elements that would normally be involved in an actual happening; a cost-saving device prepared by those in charge of special effects.

MISE-EN-SCENE—The surroundings or environment of a stage setting.

MIX—Rerecording on one track a balanced combination of the three separate tracks of voices, effects, and music and giving each the desired level of volume.

MIXER—A person who mixes sound.

MONTAGE—A juxtaposition of abbreviated shots, optical effects, or both that produce an effect, such as a sense of the passage of time, the distorted mind of a drug addict, etc.

MOS—"Mit out sound": the actual utterance of a well-known German cinematographer that took root; silent shots or sequences (filmed without synchronized sound).

MOVIEOLA—A machine used by editors for viewing the picture with sound; can be run forward or backward by foot pressure (*Movieola* is a brand name).

MUSIC TRACK—A track on which music alone is recorded.

OBLIGATORY SCENE—A confrontation at some point in the play—in many cases, the climax—which has been promised or indicated as a necessary conclusion to the earlier behavior of the parties involved.

OFF SCREEN (OS)—The designation for any element or character present in the action but visually excluded by the camera angle.

OVERHEAD SHOT—Looking down at a subject, for instance, at a pool table.

OVER THE SHOULDER—Shooting from behind one person over his shoulder to see the face of another when two characters face one another.

PAN—The movement of the camera, on a pivot, from side to side on a horizontal plane.

PAYOFF—An inevitable result for which the audience has been prepared.

POINT OF VIEW (POV)—A shot in which the camera becomes the eyes of a particular character, seeing what the character sees.

PROCESS—A shot in which the foreground (FG) action is played on a stage while the background (BG) action is rear-projected on a translucent screen from behind.

PROPERTIES (PROPS)—The decorations and furnishings on a set.

REVERSE ANGLE—An angle the opposite of the one that precedes it.

RUSHES—The uncut film, as it was shot, which is printed for viewing by the filmmakers; also called "the dailies" because the film is usually viewed the day after it was shot; the object is to check for errors before the set is taken down.

SCENARIO—The general outline or form of a script; rarely used in TV or film today.

SECOND UNIT—A minimal camera crew that photographs parts of a film that do not require the use of the main cast; usually a cost-saving device.

SEGUE—The transition from one sound or scene to another (pronounced sa'gwa).

SEQUENCE—A series of related shots that together constitute a dramatic step in the development of the plot.

SETUP—A new setup occurs any time the camera angle changes.

SHOOTING SCHEDULE—The day-out-of-days assignment board constructed by the production manager for the sequential shooting of the screen-play or teleplay.

SHOOTING SCRIPT—The final script used for principal photography and commonly considered to be the production blueprint.

SIMULT—Simultaneously.

SMASH CUT—An abrupt cut in the action from one critical moment to the next used by a screenwriter to communicate a sense of pressure or urgency to an editor or reader.

SOUND STAGE—The area of a building in which sound film is shot.

SPINE—The backbone of a play, the basic plot.

SPLICE—Sealing two pieces of film together.

SPLIT SCREEN—The effect of wiping half the picture off the screen and replacing that half with another picture.

STOCK SHOT—Footage that is general in nature and may be used to supply mood, atmosphere, or details of imagery; collected and stored in libraries, such film may be rented for a fee in order to avoid the necessity of shooting it.

STORY ANALYST—A specialist who synopsizes, analyzes, criticizes, and assesses the value of teleplays and screenplays.

STORYBOARD—A series of sketches of key incidents in a film's proposed action that is arranged on a board with captions to indicate the visual development.

STORYLINE—The play's story development.

STRUCTURE—The organized blocks of dramatic action of a plot.

SUBPLOT—A separate story involving collateral characters that is parallel to the main plot; although it progresses with the story, one could as easily dispense with it and still have the full story.

SUPERIMPOSE (SUPER)—A laboratory process in which one image on film is printed on another.

SWISH PAN—A panning shot that is so rapid it creates a blurred effect; usually used for transitions from one shot to the next.

SYNCHRONIZATION (SYNC)—Matching the audio to the video so that dialogue or sounds occur at the same moment as their visual counterparts.

TAG LINE—The closing speech in a scene.

TAKE—A filming of a shot, from the time the camera rolls (begins filming) until it stops.

THREE SHOT—A camera angle including three characters in the action.

TILT (UP or DOWN)—The movement of the camera up or down on its axis vertically.

TRANSITION—Any effect—music, sound, or optical—that links the sequential elements of a film.

TRUCKING SHOT—Moving the camera on its dolly to follow the action on a lateral plane.

TWO SHOT—A camera angle including two characters in the action.

UP—Increase of volume of sound.

VIDEO—The video portion of a motion picture.

VIEWER—An enlarging unit by which film can be more closely examined.

VOICE OVER (VO)—When the one who is speaking is not on the screen (not seen).

WIDE SHOT—A "wide-angle" shot including the maximum of scenery or action for scenic or dramatic impact.

WILD SHOT—Similar to a stock shot, but photographed by the film's own production unit.

WIPE—An optical effect with two succeeding shots by which the second wipes the first off the screen.

WORK PRINT—A print of the picture used for cutting and editing so that the original negative is not marred in the process of making corrections.

WRAP—The end of a day's shooting.

ZOOMAR—A lens that achieves the effect of moving toward (ZOOM IN) or away (ZOOM OUT) from a subject without the camera physically moving.

INDEX

action, 25–26, 30, 34–35, 214. *See also* plot

acts: Acts I, II, and III, 24–25, 31–32, 43, 45, 59; in *Claire Serrat*, 32–33, 44; and tag lines and curtain lines, 59, 208, 214; in television, 24, 59; and theoretical premise, 31–32

adaptation: nature of, 3; and plot, 23; rights to, 5–6, 206; stories worthy of, 30; and theme, 21. *See also* plays; scripts; writers

adapter. *See* writers

agents, 6

Allwyn, Robert (character), 16, 44, 52

angles. *See* camera angles and shots

animation, 207

answer print, 207

antagonist: in *Claire Serrat*, 40–41; and conflict, 11–12; and plot development, 25, 31; in premise, 31, 34; questions regarding, 14. *See also* protagonist; Thibaut, Martin

art director, 207

audience: and conflict, 12–13, 26; emotions of, 25–27, 30–31, 34, 40, 43, 56–57; nature of, 9, 29; questions concerning, 201–204; and suspense, 24; and theme, 20; witholding information from, 27. *See also* emotions

audio, 207

background (BG), 207

back light, 207

back lot, 207

backstory, 9, 14, 24, 35, 41, 206, 209

beat, 207

Bentham, Jeremy, 12

blimp, 207

blowup, 207

boom, 208

budgets, 60

business, 208

camera angles and shots: extensive discussion of, 62–63; in treatment, 45; unnecessary, 60–61, 204. *See also angles and shots by name*

camera operators, 62, 210

Candy (character), 16, 52

caper, 208

capital letters, 45, 62, 64

cause and effect, 38–40, 44, 206

characters: audience involvement with, 7, 29, 31, 56–59; central or main, 3, 19, 21, 39; development of, 35–41; and dialogue, 27–28, 56–59; elimination of, 42, 204; and premise, 34; and plot, 23, 25; problems of, 9–10; questions concerning, 201–204; reactions of, 10; in script, 64; and theme, 20–22; thoughts of, 3; traits of, 7,

37–38; values of, 31, 34–36, 41, 43, 59, 202, 205. *See also* antagonist; protagonist; *characters by name*

chronology, 7, 23, 35, 45. *See also* time

Claire Serrat: acquisition of rights for, 5; character development and, 40–42; and flashbacks, 28; and plot of screenplay, 19; premise of, 32–33; questions concerning, 19; screenplay of, 71–197; screenplay format of, 61; subtext of, 18–19; summary of 15–18; theme of 19–20; treatment of, 46–55. *See also characters by name*

climax: identifying, 12; in plot, 25, 43–44, 203, 205; and premise, 31–34

close, 62

close shot (CS), 62, 63, 208

close–up (CU), 62, 64, 208

comedy, 34, 42

composite, 208

composition, 208

conflict: freedom versus captivity, 19; issues of, 6, 11–12, 24–25, 32, 34, 36, 44–45, 202, 205; Person versus Person, Nature, or Self, 11–12, 14, 36; and premise, 31–34; and problems, 26, 34; questions concerning, 14, 202, 205; resolution of, 9–12, 20, 44; significance of, 12; and violence, 29; woman versus man, 19, 32

confrontation, 208. *See also* conflict

continuity, 208

contractions, 57

contrast, 208

conversation. *See* dialogue

copyrights: acquiring, 3–6, 206; Copyright Office, Library of Congress, 5

crane, 208

credit, 208

crisis, 25, 31–34, 43, 203, 205. *See also* conflict

culminating events, 26–27, 202

curtain line, 59, 208

cut, 63, 208

cutaway, 208

cutback, 208

cutting, 208

cyclorama, 208

danger, 29. *See also* conflict; suspense

day for night, 209

denouement, 209

deus ex machina, 209

dialects, 58–59

dialogue: and adaptation, 3; extensive discussion of, 56–59; manners of speech and, 35; questions concerning, 203–204; and theme, 20, 205

dissolve, 63, 209

dolly (in and out), 63, 209

down, 209

drama: defined, 31; and dramatic action, 30–31, 34; nature of, 29, 57; and relationship to novel, 35, 42; structure of, 3; values of, 61

dramatic variability, 10–11

dramatist. *See* writers

dub, 209

editor, 209

effects, 209

emotions: of audience, 25–27, 30–31, 34, 201–204; anxiety, 36, 203; of characters, 56–58; defined, 30; and dialogue, 58–59; guilt, 8–9; versus intellect, 10; sympathy, empathy, and antipathy, 9, 25, 34, 43–44, 201–203

establish (EST), 209

exposition, 27–28, 35, 202, 205, 209

extreme close–up (ECU), 21, 62, 209

fade (in or out), 63, 209

fantasy, 8–9

farce, 42

favoring angles, 63, 209

Fenwick, Dr. John (character), 15, 16, 47

flashback, 24, 28, 202, 210
focus: of camera, 210; of play, 14
follow, 210
foreground (FG), 210
frame, 210
freeze frame, 210
full shot (FS), 62, 210

gaffer, 62, 210
gag, 210
gimmick, 210
Goldwyn, Samuel, 20, 22
grips, 62, 210
group shot, 62, 210

hand held, 210
head–on shot, 210
high angles, 63, 210
high–key lighting, 210
hook, 210

imagination, 7
inky–dink, 210
insert, 210
internalization, 3
issue of conflict. *See* conflict, issues of

jeopardy, 211
jump cut, 211

key light, 211

lap dissolve, 211
lead, 211. *See also* characters, central or
      main
legal issues. *See* copyrights
lighting setup, 211
limbo, 211
lip sync, 211
location, 211
long shot (LS), 62, 211
loop, 211
low angles, 63, 211

macro shot, 211
main title, 211

master scenes, 61. *See also* scenes
matching, 211
matching shot, 212
matte, 212
Medical College of Pennsylvania, 5
medium shot (MS), 62, 212
melodramas, 35
mind, 8–9. *See also* emotions;
      psychology
miniature, 212
mise–en–scène, 212
mix, 212
mixer, 212
montage, 212
MOS, 212
motivation, 14, 19, 43–44
movieola, 212
moving shot, 63
music track, 212

narrator, 27
novels and stories: choice of, 10, 205;
      novels versus plays and short
      stories, 3–4, 6–7; plot of, 42, 45,
      58; questions concerning, 43;
      reducing, 6, 19, 21, 34, 204;
      rereading, 39–40; rights and, 5–6;
      summarizing, 14; and themes, 21

obligatory scene, 212
off screen (OS), 212
One Flew Over the Cuckoo's Nest, 28
opposing forces: in premise, 31, 34;
      questions regarding, 14, 202; and
      suspense, 24; types of, 11–12, 14,
      36. *See also* antagonist; conflict
options, 5
overhead shots, 63, 212
over the shoulder angles, 63, 212

pan, 63, 212
payoff, 212
Person versus Nature, Person, or Self,
      11–12, 14, 36
plays: audience involvement with, 3, 7,
      9, 25–26, 30–31, 34, 40, 43, 56–

57; characters and , 35–41; dialogue in, 56–59, 205; engine of, 11; example of treatment for, 46–55; original versus adaptation, 21; plot of, 23–29, 42; premise of, 30–34; questions concerning, 43; reading versus performance of, 8; and theme, 20–22; versus novels, 9. *See also* adaptation; novels and stories

playwright. *See* writers

plot: acts in, 24–25; complications of, 27; and dialogue, 56, 59; in melodramas, 35; revision of, 6; structure of, 23–25, 204; subplots and, 6, 24, 42, 204, 214; unity of action of, 25; what to avoid in, 26. *See also* acts

point of departure, 6, 12, 33–43, 201, 206

point of view (POV), 25, 27, 44, 63, 204, 213

premise, 10, 30–34, 206

pretense, 6–7

problem. *See* conflict

process, 213

properties (props), 213

protagonist: and audience involvement, 31; conflict and problems of, 6, 9, 11–13, 23, 34, 38, 43; and plot development, 23–28; questions regarding, 14, 40, 201–202

psychology, 8–9, 12, 16, 35–36. *See also* emotions; values

questions, instructional: about adaptation, 201–204; about character, 37, 40–41; importance of, 206; about novel, 14, 19; about point of departure, 43–44; about premise, 30–32; about subtext, 19

reader, 6. *See also* audience

reality, 7, 43

reverse angle, 63, 213

rewrites and revisions, 45, 204

rooting interest, 9, 26

royalties, 5

rushes, 213

scenario, 213

scenes, 3; and dialogue, 203; economy of, 6, 204; master, 61; obligatory, 212; and plot, 42, 44–45; and tag and curtain lines, 59, 208, 214; time in, 64. *See also* acts; plot

science fiction, 6

screenplays: of *Claire Serrat,* 71–197; cutting, 201; development of, 42; formats of, 60–62; length of, 6, 204; original, 206; substance of, 39. *See also* plays; scripts; writers

screenwriter. *See* writers

screenwriting, 3–4, 45. See also adaptation; plays; scripts; writers

scripts: conventions in, 45; examples of, 59, 64–67; professionalism and, 60; purpose of, 61; shooting script, 213. *See also* plays

second unit, 213

segue, 213

sequence, 213

Serrat, Claire (character): and point of departure, 44; in premise, 32–33; as protagonist, 19, 40; in summary, 15–18; in treatment, 46–55. *See also* protagonist

set designer, 63, 207

setting, 204, 205, 211, 212

setup, 213

shared screen, 63

shooting schedule, 213

shooting script, 213

short stories. *See* novels and stories

shot-for-shot technique, 61, 64–67

shots. *See* camera angles and shots

simultaneous (SIMULT), 213

smash cut, 63, 213

sounds, 45, 64, 209, 213, 215

sound stage, 213

speech. *See* dialogue

spine, 214

splice, 214
split screen, 63, 214
stock shot, 214
stories. *See* novels and stories
story analyst, 214
storyboard, 214
storyline, 214
structure, 214. *See also* acts; plot
stunts, 210
subplot. *See* plot, subplots and
subtext, 10, 18–19, 204
summary: of any story, 14; of *Claire Serrat,* 15–18
superimpose (SUPER), 63, 214
suspense, 23–25, 26, 34, 38, 202–203. *See also* conflict
suspension of disbelief, 7, 43
swish pan, 214
synchronization (sync), 214

tag line, 59, 214
take, 214
telephone, 27–28
television, 3, 204
theme: of any story, 20; of *Claire Serrat,* 19; conveying, 21–22, 205; dialogue and, 20, 22; examples of, 21; questions concerning, 14, 19; writers and, 10, 20
Thibaut, Martin (character): as antagonist, 19, 40–41, 44; in premise, 32–33; in summary, 17–18; in treatment, 46–55. *See also* antagonist
three shot, 62, 214
tilt (up or down), 63, 214
time, 6, 64, 204. *See also* chronology
titles, 27
tragedy, 42

transition, 14–22, 214
treatment, 6, 42–45, 206; example of, for *Claire Serrat,* 46–55
trucking shot, 214
two shot, 62, 215

unity, 25, 44
up, 215

values: of characters, 31, 34–36, 41, 43, 59, 202, 205; dramatic, 43, 61; as principles, 31, 35–36
verb tense, 45, 206
video, 215
viewer, 215
violence, 29, 203
voice over (VO), 215

wide shot, 215
wild shot, 215
wipe, 215
work print, 215
wrap, 215
writers: adapters, 3–4, 10, 21, 45, 58; and camera language and screenplay format, 60–62; and cheating audience, 27; and developing characters, 35–41; and dialogue, 56–59; and excessive direction, 58–59, 62; motivation of, 20; obligations of, 62; plot techniques of, 23–24, 29; point of view and, 20; screenwriters, 3–4, 204; skill of, 21, 24, 27–28, 35, 45; and theme, 20–21; work of, 56. *See also* questions, instructional
Wylie, Ida Alexa Ross, 5, 35

zoom (in or out), 63, 215
Zoomar lens, 63, 215